Praise for *Mistreatment in the Workplace*:

"At last, an excellent guidebook, rich in illustrative cases, that competently tells human relations practitioners and managers how to prevent, detect, diagnose, and redirect perceived unfairness in work situations."

Evert Van de Vliert, Professor Emeritus, University of Groningen, and recipient of the Lifetime Achievement Award from the International Association for Conflict Management

"Olson-Buchanan and Boswell have done an excellent job in merging state-of-the art science with clear and much needed recommendations for dealing with mistreatment at work. *Mistreatment in the Workplace* is a must read for academics and practitioners alike."

Carsten K.W. De Dreu, Professor of Organizational Psychology, University of Amsterdam

"This book is a must read for anyone interested in managing a critical issue in organizations: mistreament. Olson-Buchanan and Boswell, leading scholars in the field, have provided the best practices – based on the best science – for how to prevent mistreatments and manage them once they occur. Vivid examples, systematic analyses, and thoughtful advice make this a truly outstanding book."

Michele J. Gelfand, Professor of Psychology, University of Maryland

D1329915

Talent Management Essentials

Series Editor: Steven G. Rogelberg, Ph.D
Professor and Director Organizational Science, University of North Carolina – Charlotte

Senior Advisory Board:
- Eric Elder, Ph.D., Director, Talent Management, Corning Incorporated
- Bill Macey, Ph.D., Chief Executive Officer, Valtera Corporation
- Cindy McCauley, Ph.D., Senior Fellow, Center for Creative Leadership
- Elaine Pulakos, Ph.D., Chief Operating Officer, Personnel Decisions Research Institutes,
- Doug Reynolds, Ph.D., Vice President, Assessment Technology, Development Dimensions International
- Ann Marie Ryan, Ph.D., Professor, Michigan State University
- Lise Saari, Ph.D., Direct, Global Workforce Research, IBM
- John Scott, Ph.D., Vice President, Applied Psychological Techniques, Inc.
- Dean Stamoulis, Ph.D., Managing Director, Executive Assessment Practice Leader
- for the Americas, Russell Reynolds Associates

Special Features

Each volume contains a host of actual case studies, sample materials, tips, and cautionary notes. Issues pertaining to globalization, technology, and key executive points are highlighted throughout.

Titles in the Talent Management Essentials series:

Mistreatment in the Workplace

Prevention and Resolution for Managers and Organizations

Julie B. Olson-Buchanan
and Wendy R. Boswell

WILEY-BLACKWELL

A John Wiley & Sons, Ltd., Publication

Blackwell Publishing was acquired by John Wiley & Sons in February 2007. Blackwell's publishing program has been merged with Wiley's global Scientific, Technical, and Medical business to form Wiley-Blackwell.

Registered Office
John Wiley & Sons Ltd, The Atrium, Southern Gate, Chichester, West Sussex, PO19 8SQ, United Kingdom

Editorial Offices
350 Main Street, Malden, MA 02148-5020, USA
9600 Garsington Road, Oxford, OX4 2DQ, UK
The Atrium, Southern Gate, Chichester, West Sussex, PO19 8SQ, UK

For details of our global editorial offices, for customer services, and for information about how to apply for permission to reuse the copyright material in this book please see our website at www.wiley.com/wiley-blackwell.

The right of Julie B. Olson-Buchanan and Wendy R. Boswell to be identified as the authors of this work has been asserted in accordance with the Copyright, Designs and Patents Act 1988.

Library of Congress Cataloging-in-Publication Data is available for this title.

HB: 978-1-4051-7713-9
PB: 978-1-4051-7714-6

A catalogue record for this book is available from the British Library.
Icon in Case Scenario boxes © Kathy Konkle/istockphoto.com.

Set in 10.5 on 12.5 pt Minion by SNP Best-set Typesetter Ltd., Hong Kong
Printed in Singapore by Ho Printing Singapore Pte Ltd

1   2009

Table of Contents

We dedicate this book to our families
With all our love

Tim, Claire, and Beth Buchanan
David, Bonnie, and Susan Olson
JBOB

Steve, Cameron, and Gage Boswell
Tom and Carolyn Hoffman
WRB

Series Editor's Preface

The *Talent Management Essentials* series presents state-of-the-art thinking on critical talent management topics ranging from global staffing, to career pathing, to engagement, to executive staffing, to performance management, to mentoring, to real-time leadership development. Authored by leading authorities and scholars on their respective topics, each volume offers state-of-the-art thinking and the epitome of evidence-based practice. These authors bring to their books an incredible wealth of experience working with small, large, public and private organizations, as well as keen insights into the science and best practices associated with talent management.

Written succinctly and without superfluous "fluff," this series provides powerful and practical treatments of essential talent topics critical to maximizing individual and organizational health, well-being and effectiveness. The books, taken together, provide a comprehensive and contemporary treatment of approaches, tools, and techniques associated with Talent Management. The goal of the series is to produce focused, prescriptive volumes that translate the data- and practice-based knowledge of I/O psychology and Organizational Behavior into practical, "how to" advice for dealing with cutting-edge organizational issues and problems.

Talent Management Essentials is a comprehensive, practitioner-oriented series of "best practices" for the busy solution-oriented manager, executive, HR leader, and consultant. And, in its application of evidence-based practice, this series will also appeal to professors, executive MBA students, and graduate students in Organizational Behavior, Human Resources Management, and I/O Psychology.

Steven Rogelberg

Preface

A ll of us have been personally affected, in some way, by individuals feeling mistreated at work. Perhaps you experienced this as a manager where one of your higher performers became withdrawn, bitter toward coworkers, or maybe even quit after not receiving a sought-after promotion. Or, you may have a close friend or family member who became so angry or upset about a work situation in which he or she felt abused or ridiculed that it disrupted a special occasion or much-anticipated vacation. You may have personally experienced mistreatment at work such as where a colleague made rude, off-hand remarks about you (or your department) or where your manager seemed to overlook your qualifications and performance.

Whether it is called incivility, bullying, disrespect, harassment, or mistreatment, one thing is clear: the way individuals are treated at work is extremely important to the individuals, others who care about those individuals, the organization, and society.

Mistreatment at Work

Why is appropriate treatment at work *so important*? To a large extent it is important because when individuals do not feel that they are treated appropriately (*mis*treatment), substantial negative conse-quences occur on many levels. First, individuals who feel mistreated at work not only suffer in terms of the basis for the mistreatment (e.g., not getting deserved rewards, public ridicule), when it is all said and done, they also often feel emotionally, psychologically, and physically drained. Second, as we know all too well from personal experience, what affects one's emotional, physical, and professional well-being will also affect the important people in our lives outside (and inside) work. Third, with respect to organizations, the media is replete with examples of organizations that are troubled, both economically and in reputation, by seemingly chronic perceptions of mistreatment. They include organizations that have had a very public employee discrimination case decided against them or organizations that are faced with widespread employee sabotage or retaliation. Finally, from a societal perspective, being treated appropriately and fairly is at the core of what we, as individuals, consider to be basic human rights.

The Purpose and Scope of the Book

Yet, important as fair treatment is to individual and organizational well-being, as organizational leaders we struggle to identify what individuals will consider to be mistreatment, as well as to determine how this mistreatment can be addressed fully in the organization or prevented in the first place. The purpose of this book is to examine how you can prevent some mistreatment, minimize other forms of mistreatment, and fully address mistreatment that does occur in your organization. The recommendations in this book rest on evidence-based best practice and empirical research.

Most books on dispute resolution focus on resolving a particular instance of mistreatment, but do not address how experiencing mistreatment (or being accused of it) will affect the working relationship of the parties involved after the mistreatment is "resolved" nor how to prevent or minimize mistreatment in the organization. We consider particular instances to be only part of the picture, and we approach the problem differently. Specifically, we explain what else needs to be done after the mistreatment is resolved to more fully address its consequences and to prevent a spiral of mistreatment or chronic mistreatment from occurring, and we also recommend practical ways of preventing or minimizing mistreatment throughout the organization.

There are numerous well-crafted books that have focused on using Alternative Dispute Resolution (ADR) approaches to resolving claims of mistreatment instead of the court system. Again this book is different. It does not focus on these external approaches. Instead it focuses on how dispute resolution methods such as mediation or arbitration might be used *internally* within your organization to resolve mistreatment concerns successfully.

Background and Development of the Book

Together, we have over 30 years of experience in the field. Julie B. Olson-Buchanan started in this field 18 years ago when she initiated her dissertation at the University of Illinois, Urbana-Champaign, on the antecedents and consequences of voicing discontent in organizations. Wendy R. Boswell began her work over 12 years ago when she was a PhD student at Cornell University's School of Industrial and Labor Relations. We started collaborating on field research in the area, and since that time we have published a number of articles related to experiencing and addressing mistreatment in organizations. In addition to our scholarly work we have both acted as consultants to several different organizations, providing expertise in the prevention and resolution of mistreatment in organizations. Finally, we have provided managerial and executive training to numerous organizations on the issues discussed in this book, as well as expert witness testimony relating to retaliation and voicing mistreatment in organizations.

This book is a natural outcome of the consulting experiences and research stream we have shared. Consistent with our approach to examining mistreatment in organizations in practice and in research, we have integrated the findings of several different areas to prepare this book, including industrial-organizational psychology, conflict management literature, industrial relations, community psychology, social psychology, labor economics, clinical psychology, health psychology, and human resource management.

Writing this book has been a particularly interesting journey. Not only was it an opportunity to articulate the integration of so many disciplines into a practical guide, but it also gave us the opportunity to share experiences with our colleagues, friends and family. Usually when we are asked by our friends and family what we are working on, we are lucky if they are able to successfully stifle a yawn when we answer. The precise opposite was the case in this instance. Invariably, whenever we explained that we were writing a book about mistreatment, the other person would immediately respond with a comment like "Have I got an example for you!" or "I'd like to tell you about this company I used to work for, you would find it very interesting."

Colleagues who were aware that we were working on the book introduced areas that were new to us, but very much needed to be a part of the book. In addition, our colleagues (whom we have the good fortune to call friends as well!) shared expertise and experiences that made the book much richer.

We are particularly fortunate to be able to use real examples throughout the book. Most of them have come from our consulting or in-house experiences, and a few examples were contributed by our colleagues and other friends. You will find that we only identify organizations when they have information about a certain procedure or approach in the public domain, such as a website or in print. In those examples that are identified by name we have usually changed the names of those involved or the setting to protect privacy.

On a more personal note, some of the examples in this book come from the experiences of people who are particularly dear to us. We have seen first-hand how unresolved and chronic mistreatment in organizations can take a serious and enduring toll on those involved, as well as those who care about those involved. It is our hope that sharing these examples will help to prevent mistreatment in your organizations.

Structure of the Book

We have structured this book to reflect, in part, the progressive cycle in which mistreatment is experienced and addressed in the workplace. We introduce the topic (Chapter 1) by discussing the consequences of workplace mistreatment, including the costs to the organization and the individuals involved. We emphasize that, though there are considerable negative consequences of mistreatment in the workplace, the purpose of this book is to illustrate how prevalent, costly mistreatment can be avoided.

In Chapter 2 we define the full scope of mistreatment and provide a discussion of the various types (or aliases) of mistreatment. Contractual and legal definitions are also discussed. This chapter concludes with a description of the process by which individuals "make sense" of a situation potentially involving some type of mistreatment. This sense-making process is a critical step in the cycle, as the ultimate outcome is that the employee will conclude whether, and if so how, he or she was mistreated.

We then focus our discussion on how to prevent and address such mistreatment in the workplace, beginning with Chapter 3 where we discuss how your organization can use workplace scanning to identify potential and nascent issues so that they can be addressed early. In Chapter 4 we discuss how several human resource/work practices including the role of employee selection and training, reward structures, managerial development, and disciplinary actions can be used to foster a work environment in which mistreatment is prevented or addressed early on, before it develops into a larger problem.

Designing and implementing an effective dispute resolution system is a key factor in preventing mistreatment in the workplace as well as an important means to address or resolve mistreatment that has already occurred. In Chapter 5 we discuss how to approach designing a dispute resolution system that meets your organization's needs and goals. We then elaborate on and provide examples of alternative dispute resolution options (Chapter 6). Our discussion focuses on the design, implementation, and maintenance of the various informal and formal dispute resolution options, as well as the benefits and drawbacks of each. We take a "best practice" perspective in Chapter 7, discussing the elements of a state-of-the-art dispute resolution system as broad, deep, and integrated. We conclude this chapter by offering suggestions for how such a state-of-the-art system could be modified for smaller organizations.

The next two chapters reflect the fact that addressing workplace mistreatment does not end after a particular issue has been "resolved." Indeed, without proper auditing or follow-up, a dispute resolution system may serve to exacerbate or encourage mistreatment in organizations. In Chapter 8, we discuss the on-going process of evaluating, modifying, and learning from your dispute resolution system. Measures and measurement approaches for auditing your system (given your goals for the system) are presented and how to use the information from the audit to improve your system and organizational functioning is discussed. The on-going effects of mistreatment are the focus of Chapter 9. Here we focus on how to minimize the potential damaging effects on post-mistreatment relationships (to prevent future mistreatment), repair relationships, and how to deal with unresolved mistreatment.

Our concluding chapter (Chapter 10) summarizes and integrates the preceding chapters by highlighting the overarching themes we hope readers can take away from this book.

Acknowledgments

We are indebted to so many people for supporting us in the development of this book. First we would like to thank the editor of the series, Steven Rogelberg, for inviting us to write this book and providing us with much encouragement. We would also like to thank the series editorial board, who gave us some very valuable feedback during the proposal phase as well as after the first draft of the book was complete. We are honored to be a part of this terrific series and to be in the company of such great authors.

We would like to thank Alex Colvin and James Schmidtke for their invaluable comments and suggestions on an earlier draft of this book. Their insightful, thoughtful suggestions under such tight time constraints are very much appreciated.

We would like to thank all of our colleagues whose collegiality, generosity, and support fosters a great culture in which to work. Several of our colleagues provided expertise and pointed us in the right direction when we were writing this book, including Jill Bradley, Constance Jones, James Schmidtke, Elizabeth Umphress, and Ryan Zimmerman. We thank Amanda Holley for her research assistance and Denise Biggert for her administrative support.

We are also grateful to the many people and organizations, whose identities have been masked, that are offered as examples throughout this book.

We thank our friends for their encouragement and willingness to serve as our sense-makers.

Finally, last, but not least, we thank our families for their love and support and their amazing ability to adjust to our demands as we finished this book. Kids, you can turn the volume back up now.

February 2008
Julie B. Olson-Buchanan
Fresno, California
Wendy R. Boswell
College Station, Texas

Chapter 1

Introduction

"My supervisor is a cruel bully, pure and simple. He acts unprofessionally, gossips, plays politics, you name it."

"I have a much heavier workload and have been here three years longer than a colleague who makes much more money than me."

"I was told by the division manager that I would be given a promotion, and informed the following week that the position would be posted instead."

"A subordinate was harassing several employees in the organization including me, but I was asked to endure her behavior until they figured out what to do about her."

All of these are examples of workplace mistreatment, as reported by real employees at one organization. Mistreatment in the workplace is when an employee believes that he or she has not been treated fairly in the course of performing his or her job. Note that the focus is on whether an individual *believes* he or she has been mistreated as opposed to some "objective" assessment of whether mistreatment occurred. This approach recognizes that an individual's reactions are largely driven by his or her *perceptions of mistreatment*.

There are a number of ways in which employees may feel mistreated at work, such as believing that they:

- Are not receiving a deserved
  - performance evaluation
  - raise
  - promotion
- Are being bullied by their manager
- Are being treated rudely by clients
- Are being harassed by another employee
- Are being socially excluded by other employees

Similarly, there are also a number of potential *sources* of the perceived mistreatment including one's peers, subordinates, supervisors and managers, clients and customers, and upper administration.

Just how prevalent are perceptions of mistreatment at work? The popular media is replete with examples of employees being harassed by customers, bullied by managers, and retaliated against for speaking up about unethical behavior. Empirical studies have shown that a substantial percentage of workers in the US and abroad feel they have been mistreated at work in the past year. For example, a 2000 study by Loraleigh Keashly and Karen Jagatic[1] found that 27% of employees experienced workplace mistreatment. Studies focused on psychological abuse specifically (e.g., workplace incivility, bullying, verbal abuse, hostility) indicate that as many as half of all employees report being a target, some of these subjected to such treatment weekly.[2] A report out of the National Institute for Occupational Safety and Health indicates incidents of such behavior in nine out of ten US workplaces.[3] The Equal Employment Opportunity Commission reported there were 82,792 charges of employment discrimination brought to them in 2007.[4] Note that some of these charges represent hundreds, if not thousands, of employees.

Costs of Mistreatment

One of the biggest problems for organizations is that perceived mistreatment in the workplace is very expensive. Research clearly indicates that mistreatment in the workplace takes a toll on the well-being of the individual who feels mistreated, other employees directly or indirectly involved, and the organization's bottom-line. For example, at the extreme end, recent years have witnessed litigation resulting in multi-million settlements for claims of discrimination and harassment. The costs certainly vary depending on the nature and source of the mistreatment, as well as whether and how the mistreatment is addressed. However, there are some typical costs associated with perceptions of mistreatment.[5]

Good to Know:
Costs of Workplace Mistreatment

Employee Outcomes

- Lost time and productivity
- Lower organizational commitment and loyalty
- Job withdrawal
- Acts of revenge
- Union organizing
- Higher turnover
- Retaliation
- Aggressive reactions (including workplace violence)
- Higher stress and burnout
- Higher health-related problems

Organizational Outcomes

- Decrease in production
- Lower employee morale and difficulty in recruiting
- Damage and loss of property
- Risk of unionization
- Costs of turnover
- Litigation
- Lack of information flow
- Time spent investigating and addressing
- Higher benefits (e.g., medical premiums)

Lower commitment, loyalty and morale

Research has found that employees who experience mistreatment at work are likely to have subsequently lower organizational commitment. That is, they will experience lower emotional attachment and identification with the organization. Also, mistreated employees tend to have subsequently lower loyalty to the organization, meaning, for example, they will be less willing to say positive things about the company to others. These changes in commitment and loyalty do not take place in a vacuum; as noted earlier, employees who feel mistreated will often talk with others. This talk could then shape how employees and those that they talk with view or interpret events that occur in the workplace. Our experience has shown us that chronic mistreatment of employees, in particular, has direct implications for employee morale in the workplace and organizations have a more difficult time, and likely incur more expenses, recruiting and retaining the best people.

Withdrawal and revenge

Research indicates employees change their behaviors at work after experiencing mistreatment. Some "pull back" or withdraw from work in some way. For example, they may call in sick, arrive late or leave early, or take unusually long breaks or slow down production. Again, this behavior has direct implications for an organization's bottom-line. Some employees may react by engaging in acts of revenge against the organization such as sabotage or theft. This translates into repair and replacement costs of supplies and equipment for the organization.

Job search and turnover

Research also demonstrates that employees who feel mistreated are more likely to search for other jobs and/or quit their jobs. The substantial organizational costs of organizational turnover, including separation costs (e.g., severance pay) and costs incurred by recruiting and training new employees are well documented. For example, it is estimated that employee turnover costs 50–100% of an employee's salary, dependent on the nature of the individual's job (e.g., entry level, professional level).[6] Others have suggested the cost can run as high as 200% of an employee's salary.[7] Yet, engaging in a search for alternative employment, regardless of whether it leads to turnover, is costly because the time and energy an individual spends searching could be put to other task-related uses. The process of searching for new employment may also create detachment from the current organization, further reducing commitment and fostering withdrawal behavior (e.g., tardiness).

Lost time

The experience of feeling unfairly treated at work and deciding what, if anything, to do about it, is far more time-consuming than we typically think. When individuals experience a potentially unfair scenario, they will often spend time evaluating that situation. Did my manager mean to say that? Am I over-reacting? They will also often spend time discussing or rehashing with others what happened in an attempt to understand if they have been mistreated. If they do determine they have been mistreated, they will spend more time contemplating what they should do about it (if anything at all). For the individuals, this preoccupation is likely to extend to their personal lives, taking time and emotional energy from personal or family time. For the organization, typically this process takes place during the time that would normally be devoted to completing job tasks – for the individuals who feel mistreated as well as for others with whom they discuss it. Thus, regardless of if, or how, the perceived mistreatment is resolved, it would likely, at least temporarily, result in decreased production for the organization.

 Case Scenario:
Lost Time From Mistreatment

Nicholas had over 30 years working in the insurance industry when he took a new position as a project manager for one of the largest insurance companies in the west coast. At first his relationship with his supervisor, Anna, was good. Anna was quick to praise Nicholas and introduce him around the office as a key hire. However, a few months after he began working there, Anna's behavior seemed to change. She made promises on Nicholas's behalf without consulting him – promises that, were he to honor, would mean Nicholas would have to violate internal company policy. Anna also insisted that she be present at any and all meetings which Nicholas held. She sent emails to his contacts that seemed to undermine what he was hired to do. Nicholas became increasingly uncomfortable with the situation. But he wasn't sure how to interpret it. He thought about the situation a great deal and spent a good deal of time talking with coworkers, friends, and his wife about whether Anna was not treating him appropriately and how he should or could address it. Finally, Nicholas arranged to meet with Anna to discuss his concerns. Unfortunately Anna responded to his concerns with anger. She yelled so loudly that others could hear her in the hallway. After the meeting Anna responded by pulling the reins in even tighter. As a result Nicholas spent more time discussing Anna's reaction with his peers at the company as well as his wife and his former coworkers. He also found himself going to great lengths to avoid Anna, which cost him additional productive time.

Aggressive reactions
Research on workplace violence shows that aggressive reactions (psychological or physical) from employees often stem from initial feelings of being mistreated. M. Sandy Herscovis and Julian Barling note "employees often give repeated warnings that they will commit a violent act; they often voice their concerns or feelings of perceived unfairness before they engage in such acts."[8]

Union-organizing
There is a considerable amount of evidence that some employees respond to perceived mistreatment by initiating or supporting a union-organizing campaign. Organizations are particularly vulnerable to this if there is pervasive mistreatment in the workplace. From an organization's perspective, responding to a unionization effort is costly, as is making a transition to a unionized workforce.

Retaliation
Employees who state that they have been mistreated at work often experience retaliation (i.e., are "punished") for doing so. Research demonstrates that individuals can experience negative outcomes including lower performance evaluations and lower promotion rates after they have voiced mistreatment. However, the existence and extent of retaliation seems to depend on the nature of mistreatment, the characteristics of the employee voicing it, and the way in which the employee voices it. For example, employees are more likely to be "punished" (in terms of lower performance evaluations, for example) when they reveal personal mistreatment by their supervisor than when they complain about a general work policy. Retaliation for revealing mistreatment has negative implications for the organization as well. That is, if employees are punished for speaking about unfair treatment, the organization will also suffer. Such a situation is likely to result in higher and costly employee turnover, higher litigation costs, and lower likelihood that the organization will find out about organizational problems directly from employees.

Physiological costs
There is mounting evidence from both psychological and medical research that mistreatment in the workplace results in health costs as well. Experiencing mistreatment at work has been linked with higher

stress and psychological strain. Employees are also likely to experience physiological symptoms of strain. Medical researchers report that mistreated employees are more likely to develop heart disease and experience chest pains, have a higher risk of heart attacks and produce lower self-reports of physical and mental health.[9] In addition to the detriment to an employee's well-being, an organization is likely to experience increased benefits costs in terms of higher healthcare expenses, employee absenteeism, and workers' compensation claims.

Case Scenario:
Costs of Mistreatment

A top sales representative for a multinational organization, Alexis, experienced mistreatment after she reported illegal activities that had been condoned by her manager. Although she initially discussed her concerns with her manager, the concerns were ignored and she eventually reported it to a compliance staff member and an HR manager. After the investigation, the manager and other sales representatives were told to stop the actions immediately.

After this occurred Alexis experienced retaliation. Despite her outstanding sales levels, she had subsequently lower performance ratings and a lower promotion rate. Then she experienced further retaliation in the form of discrimination after she became pregnant. Her supervisors made derogatory comments about the expenses of maternity leave to the organization and she was denied critical training opportunities. By this point, Alexis was experiencing several stress-related health problems as a result of the discrimination. Alexis again reported the problem to HR. Unfortunately this was not resolved, the retaliatory pregnancy discrimination continued, and Alexis was forced to resign. Alexis eventually decided to pursue litigation against the organization and incurred further health and social costs when her marriage suffered in the process.

After the case was over, Alexis had suffered financially, emotionally, and physically. The organization lost a top sales performer, experienced several more related lawsuits, and suffered in terms of economic costs (litigation and court awards) and negative publicity.

Is Prevalent, Costly Mistreatment Inevitable?

Given that perceived mistreatment is both prevalent and costly to organizations, a logical question to ask is, does it have to be? The short answer is *no*. Prevalent, costly mistreatment is not inevitable. Certainly some amount of conflict is to be expected when individuals are working together in organizations. Indeed, a company devoid of all conflict would be robbed of the positive benefits conflict can bring, such as new ideas and creative solutions. However, the prevalence and costs of *mistreatment* in organizations is something that can, and should, be carefully managed to enhance organizational well-being and effectiveness.

Like several other management areas, the prevention and resolution of workplace mistreatment is vulnerable to fads and anecdotal testimonials. However, adoption of these approaches may actually serve to increase mistreatment costs and even heighten threats of successful litigation. Yet there is a considerable amount of research and evidence-based practice that can be applied in organizations to minimize pervasive mistreatment and mitigate costs to the individual and organization.

The purpose of this book is to provide a blueprint for how you can design, implement, and administer a process for minimizing the incidence and costs of mistreatment in your organization and fully address mistreatment when it does occur. It is important to note that the blueprint described in this book is based on research and evidence-based practice consistent with enhancing organizational effectiveness. There are several subpurposes of the book:

- To help you understand the process by which people conclude they have been mistreated, allowing you to better anticipate and address individuals' perceptions of mistreatment.
- To show you how to create the best evidence-based practices in stand-alone and comprehensive mistreatment resolution procedures
- To show you how these practices can be modified for different types of organizations
- To show you how to use information from the resolution procedures to further enhance organizational well-being and prevent further mistreatment

- To provide a roadmap for how you can modify HR functions and Management functions to minimize the prevalence of workplace mistreatment in your organization and/or identify mistreatment early on.

Good to Know:
Key Points

- Mistreatment in the workplace is when an employee believes that he or she has not been treated fairly in the course of performing his or her job.

- Mistreatment is costly in numerous ways to both the individual who feels mistreated and the organization.
- You can take steps to minimize pervasive mistreatment and mitigate costs to the individual and your organization.

Chapter 2

Concluding Mistreatment

Understanding how employees conclude they have been mistreated is key to resolving and preventing mistreatment in the workplace. In this book, we primarily focus on *perceptions of mistreatment*. Accordingly, we recognize that mistreatment may be one person's point of view, and that this point of view may or may not be shared by others. As noted earlier, it is important to recognize that the costly consequences of mistreatment (individual and organizational) are driven by an *individual's perceptions of mistreatment*.

In this chapter, the full scope of what falls under the umbrella of mistreatment will be defined and illustrated to better enable you to anticipate and ultimately address mistreatment in the workplace. First, a caveat: These types of mistreatment are not mutually exclusive and may have considerable overlap. Several of the examples provided below may also be appropriate to more than one type of mistreatment. The importance of contractual and legal definitions of mistreatment will also be discussed. We conclude with a discussion of the role sense-making plays in how an employee arrives at a conclusion of mistreatment.

Scope of Mistreatment

Mistreatment is an umbrella term that encompasses several different but specific types. Although some of these have been discussed as stand-alone topics in the media, practice, and empirical studies, they share one thing in common: all focus on an employee feeling unfairly treated at work. Many of these types of mistreatment have legal definitions as well, which will also be discussed.

Inequitable (Distributive) Treatment

One general type of mistreatment is distributive inequity, or not receiving a deserved outcome at work. This outcome could be anything of value to the employee, including a raise, performance evaluation, training opportunity, promotion, task assignment, or recognition. J. S. Adams' well-known Equity Theory is relevant here. That is, this type of mistreatment includes an individual's perception that the outcomes he or she received from an employer (e.g., pay, recognition) are not in proportion to the inputs he or she contributed (e.g., effort, performance) when compared with the outcomes for similar inputs received by some other individual (e.g., a coworker, someone with a similar job elsewhere). There is an overwhelming amount of empirical field and laboratory evidence that individuals are highly motivated to address or resolve inequity; that is, to restore equity It is important to note that many of the ways employees address inequity (e.g., decreasing performance, increased absences) are, as discussed earlier, costly to organizations.

The causes of inequitable treatment are varied. It is important to stress that the value ascribed to the inputs and outcomes are the *employee's perceptions.* An employee may, consequently, have a higher evaluation of his or her inputs than the organization does. For example, the employee may consider his or her educational degree to be highly valuable, while the employee's manager does not consider the degree to be relevant. Similarly, the value an employee may place on an outcome he or she receives from an employer, such as recognition or opportunities for travel, may be less than the value ascribed to it by the manager or organization. Second, the person to whom the employee is comparing his or her ratio of inputs and outcomes can play an important role. The employee may be comparing himself or herself to a worker in another organization or a coworker in the same organization about whom his or her manager has little or different information. Third, organizational constraints can play a large role. The organization may have limited opportunity to reward with monetary compensation (e.g., because of the union environment or the state of the economy) and instead rewards with recognition, etc., yet the employee values monetary compensation over all other rewards.

Examples:
Inequitable Mistreatment

- Applying for a promotion, and not receiving it although someone less qualified does receive it.
- Being paid less than the market rate for the job.
- Missing out on a training session because you had to manage the office, while others attended the session.
- Consistently being assigned a task that requires you to work with the most difficult people when others are given more desirable assignments.

Unfair Processes and Policies

Another kind of mistreatment includes perceptions that a manager's or organization's processes and policies are not fair or that the way the processes and policies are implemented is not fair, or even that a manager or organization does not actually follow its own policy. The work on procedural justice is particularly relevant.[1] An individual may feel mistreated because of how the decision is made or because of some features of a particular policy or system. Several features of procedures have been identified as important to individuals in making fairness decisions of this type,[2] including whether he or she has voice (or can express his or her opinions), whether the procedure or policy is consistently applied, whether the procedure or policy is affected by bias, and whether the procedure or policy is ethical.

We know from our experience and empirical research that there are a number of ways by which an employee might perceive there to be unfair processes and policies in the workplace. The processes and policies may not be explicitly communicated, and the employee may not be able to piece together how the process or policy works. There may be explicit, well-communicated policies and procedures, but the employee's manager may not actually follow them for all employees, or may circumvent them in some way. Or, there may not actually be any explicit policies or procedures at all. The policies themselves may be missing some key elements, such as the opportunity for employees to give feedback or voice. Also, the policies or procedures may be particularly vulnerable to managerial bias.

Examples:
Unfair Processes and Policies Mistreatment

- An employee is not allowed to explain what happened before being disciplined.
- A manager does not follow the promotion policy when making decisions involving friends.
- A manager does not follow the organization's seniority-based vacation policy and instead bases vacation decisions on "first-come, first-serve."

Incivility

Another type of mistreatment is being treated rudely or disrespectfully in the workplace. The work on interactional justice is relevant here. Interactional justice comprises two types – informational and interpersonal justice. *Informational justice* is focused on facilitating perceptions of fair treatment by providing explanations of the use of certain procedures or of how outcomes were distributed. Providing candid and thorough explanations is particularly critical to preventing mistreatment, a specific focus of Chapter 9. *Interpersonal justice* is defined as whether an individual is treated with dignity and respect, and is thus of most relevance when we think about workplace incivility. There has been a rise in workplace incivility, with the overwhelming majority of employees reporting it as being a problem in their workplace. Workplace incivility is defined as: "low intensity deviant behavior with ambiguous intent to harm the target, in violation of workplace norms for mutual respect. Uncivil behaviors are characteristically rude and discourteous, displaying a lack of regard for others."[3]

What causes workplace incivility? Workplace incivility may result from a number of different sources. There is some evidence that loosened societal and organizational norms have served to blur the distinction between acceptable and unacceptable behavior at work. That is, organizations do not have a clear line drawn between what is acceptable and what is unacceptable. Managers, and organizations as a whole, can contribute to workplace incivility by providing examples which indicate that disrespectful, rude behaviors are acceptable. For example, we know of several organizations where the top CEO is notorious for his or her rude, inappropriate comments. Also, managers and organizations' unwillingness to address incivility, when it does occur, leads to more incivility in the workplace.

Examples: Incivility in the Workplace Mistreatment
• Rude language or tone • Name-calling • Non-verbal behavior such as eye-rolling or smirking • Starting rumors or gossiping

Bullying

A related type of mistreatment, is bullying. The Workplace Bullying Institute defines workplace bullying as repeated health-harming mistreatment of one or more targets by one or more perpetrators. Bullying can take the form of verbal abuse, offensive conduct that is threatening, humiliating, or intimidating, or work interference such as sabotage that prevents the target from getting work done. It is similar to incivility, but is generally considered higher in intensity because it includes some level of intent. Although the term "bully" may conjure up an image of the playground bully who steals lunch money with the threat (or promise) of physical violence, in the workplace context it is much more broadly used. Indeed, research has found that the most common type of bullying behavior is "covert nonverbal attack on task."[4] This is perhaps best exemplified by an individual withholding job information from someone who needs it. That is to say that sometimes the *absence* of certain behaviors (e.g., not including someone in important meetings, not passing on critical messages) constitutes bullying. It is estimated that 37% of US workers have been the targets of workplace bullying, with another 12% witnessing the behavior.[5]

Clearly, individuals experiencing such threatening, hostile, belittling, and outright abusive behavior will experience adverse effects including many of the psychological and behavioral reactions discussed previously. Organizations also experience substantial costs in the form of retaliation, lower productivity, higher absences and benefits costs as well as higher turnover. While "bullies" can take any form, managers and supervisors are often the perpetrators, leaving targets to feel powerless and afraid to seek redress.

Bullying may occur out of jealousy, desire for power, or even out of insecurity. There is some evidence that individuals who were victims of bullying are more likely to bully others. Of course, some bullies may have antisocial personality disorders (e.g., borderline personality disorders, narcissism, Machiavellianism). Like workplace incivility, bullying in the workplace often occurs because the organizational culture allows it to occur by failing to draw the line between appropriate and inappropriate behavior. A workplace that encourages excessive competition, perfectionism, motivation through fear, and/or winning "at all costs" is ripe for bullies to thrive.

Examples:
Bullying Mistreatment

- A supervisor aggressively crowds an employee's physical space – stands close to make the employee nervous, hovers over him or her, blocks the doorway, etc.
- An employee is isolated from the information he or she needs to perform the job – including being left off email circulation lists and not being invited to attend important training or staff meetings.
- A manager has angry outbursts; screaming, cursing, and throwing items.
- An employee walks by a co-worker's desk multiple times a day making derogatory remarks and epithets under his breath.
- A supervisor constantly changes performance standards and then harshly criticizes the employee for failing to perform.

Organizational Wrongdoing

Another possible form of mistreatment is organizational wrongdoing. According to whistle-blowing researchers, Janet Near and Marcia Miceli,[6] organizational wrongdoing includes any illegal, immoral, and illegitimate actions taken by members of an organization. In many instances of organizational wrongdoing, there may not be an individual employee, per se, who experiences mistreatment. Instead, stockholders, consumers, or society as a whole may be the most affected. However, depending on its nature, the wrongdoing could result in individual mistreatment. For example, sexual harassment, an illegal activity, would also be a type of mistreatment against the individual who experienced it. Similarly, if an individual was pressured to keep quiet about an illegal activity and threatened with retaliation if he or she did not, then this would be considered individual mistreatment.

Examples:
Organizational Wrongdoing

- Legally prohibited discrimination and harassment, such as
  - Sexual harassment, racial harassment, religious harassment, etc.
  - Illegal employment discrimination based on a race, national origin, gender, disability, etc.
- Taking adverse action (i.e., retaliation) against an individual for
  - Filing a charge of discrimination
  - Participating in a discrimination proceeding
  - Otherwise opposing discrimination
- Retaliation against an individual for engaging in whistle-blowing for organizational wrongdoing such as
  - Unsafe work practices
  - Accounting fraud
  - Industrial espionage (e.g., bribery, theft of trade secrets, technological surveillance)
  - Pollution (e.g., Illegal dumping)

Specific types of organizational wrongdoing constituting individual mistreatment are discussed in more detail next.

Harassment

Although the Merriam-Webster dictionary defines "harass" as "to create an unpleasant or hostile situation especially by uninvited and unwelcome verbal or physical conduct,"[7] making it fairly similar to incivility and bullying, we also often think of it in terms of its legal definition. For example, the Equal Employment Opportunity Commission (EEOC) defines harassment as "unwelcome conduct that is based on race, color, sex, religion, national origin, disability, and/or age. Harassment becomes unlawful where 1) enduring the offensive conduct becomes a condition of continued employment, or 2) the conduct is severe or pervasive enough to create a work environment that a reasonable person would consider intimidating, hostile, or abusive."[8] The number of harassment claims have steadily increased over the years. In 2007, there were 27,112 claims of workplace harassment filed with the EEOC, which resulted in nearly 66 million dollars of award benefits (not including those awarded through litigation).[9] However, it is important to note that harassment can take other forms, not necessarily prohibited by US law, as well, focusing on such things as political affiliation, geographic origin within a country, physical appearance, or even style of dress. The key characteristic is that an employee feels tormented by the persistent verbal or physical behaviors of others in their workplace.

Examples:
Harassment

- An employee is referred to by a racial slur.
- A manager repeatedly makes lewd jokes and sexual references in front of other employees.
- An employee is the recipient of several public "pranks" and "jokes" by fellow employees, all of which focus on the employee's poor memory. The pranks and jokes continue even after the employee asks them to stop.

One particular type of harassment, sexual harassment, has received a considerable amount of attention in the public media and numerous other literatures. Sexual harassment is defined by the EEOC as "Unwelcome sexual advances, requests for sexual favors, and other verbal or physical conduct of a sexual nature constitutes sexual harassment when submission to or rejection of this conduct explicitly or implicitly affects an individual's employment, unreasonably interferes with an individual's work performance or creates an intimidating, hostile or offensive work environment."[10] There have been numerous high-profile examples of sexual harassment claims involving public figures. The EEOC reported over 12,000 charges that were filed in 2006.[11]

There are a number of different explanations for why people harass one another. As noted above, harassment overlaps with both incivility and bullying, so those explanations apply here as well. With respect to sexual harassment in particular, there is certainly some belief that sexual harassment occurs because of misunderstandings over what may be considered offensive. However, research evidence supports the idea that harassers engage in sexual harassment to create, maintain, or assert power over others in the workplace.

Discrimination
Another type of organizational wrongdoing is discrimination. This form of mistreatment exists when an employee believes that he or she has been treated differently because of some prejudice against him or her or because some practice or policy disproportionately works to the disadvantage of a group to which he or she belongs. This

---

Examples:
Discrimination

- A single woman believes she is given more work by her manager and is asked to work more overtime because of her marital status.
- A transportation company has a policy which sets a minimum height and weight for long-haul truck drivers. An Hispanic male believes this is discriminatory because it disproportionately screens out certain demographic groups from getting the higher-paying jobs.
- A manager thinks he was denied a promotion because his manager is prejudiced against his religion.
- A male nurse believes he is excluded from social activities with other nurses because of his gender.

mistreatment might include several of the types previously described, such as not receiving deserved conditions of employment (inequitable treatment described above), unfair policies or procedures, or may be along the lines of incivility, bullying, or harassment. However, it is important to note that with discrimination, the employee feels the mistreatment occurred as a result of the fact that he or she belongs to a particular group (e.g., racial, religious, political).

Why do people discriminate against one another? There is some research evidence that some people may prefer to create and maintain hierarchies between different groups in the workplace (and in society in general).[12] Such individuals engage in discriminatory acts to dominate over individuals in other groups, thereby maintaining these hierarchical differences. There is also evidence that individuals develop prejudices against other groups because of a previous (or ongoing) competition for scarce resources. Individuals may carry this prejudice into the workplace or may even develop it on the job if different groups appear to vie for limited resources.

Discrimination may involve a legally protected characteristic (e.g., race, disability). Legal definitions are discussed in more detail in the following section of this chapter. However, it is important to note, that an individual may perceive discrimination based on a characteristic not necessarily protected by the law, yet this would still constitute perceived mistreatment.

Case Scenario:
When "Legal" Discrimination May Be Perceived as Mistreatment

Lynn is the most experienced and consistently the "top salesperson" at the car dealership. A position for a sales manager becomes available and Lynn applies. The district manager does not promote Lynn, citing that he "doesn't want to lose his top performer." Lynn feels she has been discriminated against simply because she does her job so well.

Retaliation
Retaliation is an adverse action taken against an employee for opposing a discriminatory practice, participating in a discrimination proceeding, or for whistle-blowing against an organization engaged in

unsafe, illegal, or unethical practices. Retaliation may prevent the employee or other employees from engaging in concerted activity or protected conduct The legal issues concerning retaliation are discussed further in the section Legal and Contractual Aspects of Mistreatment below.

Examples:
Retaliation Mistreatment

- An employee is threatened with termination if she continues to complain about poor working conditions.
- An employee is terminated for informing the EPA about the organization's illegal dumping practice.
- An employee is denied training opportunities because she raised a discrimination concern about the travel policy.

Legal and Contractual Aspects of Mistreatment

Whether and how an organization responds to or prevents mistreatment is not entirely within the organization's discretion. That is, some forms of mistreatment are expressly prohibited by legislation or contractual agreement. Being familiar with these statutes will help you to anticipate general legal concerns about claims of mistreatment and prompt you to seek legal counsel appropriately. In this section, the major pieces of United States legislation will be identified followed by a brief discussion of international legislation. Finally, the relation between collective bargaining agreements, perceived mistreatment, and resolving mistreatment will be discussed. Note that a detailed discussion of relevant legislation and case law is beyond the scope of this book. Instead, this section is provided to familiarize you with the general legal context for some forms of mistreatment, and you should consult additional materials for your particular situation.[13]

United States Equal Employment Opportunity (EEO) Legislation

The term "Equal Employment Opportunity" legislation is used to describe the host of statutes designed to ensure equal access to employment by prohibiting certain kinds of discrimination. The following table shows some of the major pieces of EEO legislation (left side of table) and what mistreatment is expressly prohibited by the statute as well as how it is has been interpreted (center of table) and which employers must abide by it (right side of table). Note that discrimination does not need to be intentional for it to be considered discrimination. That is, seemingly neutral practices such as minimum physical requirements may have the effect of discriminating against a group of individuals.

Good to Know

Equal Employment Opportunity Legislation	Prohibited Mistreatment as defined (and interpreted)	Applicable to
• Equal Pay Act of 1963	• Sex-based wage discrimination for substantially equal work	• Employers in Inter-State Commerce
• Civil Rights Act of 1964, Title VII	• Discrimination in employment conditions on the basis of sex, race, national origin, religion, or color (including sexual harassment)	• Employers with 15+ employees • State and local governments • Employment agencies • Labor organizations
• Age Discrimination in Employment Act (1967, amended 1986)	• Discrimination against employees (in conditions of employment) 40 years and older	• Employers with 20+ employees • Employment agencies • Labor organizations • Federal government

• Executive Order 11478	• Prohibits discrimination on the basis of sex, race, color, national origin or religion	• Federal Government • Federal contractors with $10,000+
• Vocational Rehabilitation Act (1973)	• Prohibits discrimination against an "otherwise qualified handicapped individual"	• Agencies, contractors and subcontractors with $2500+ of federal contracts
• Americans with Disabilities Act (1990)	• Workplace discrimination against disabled employees (or potential employees)	• Employers with 15+ employees
• Civil Rights Act of 1991	• Same as Civil Rights Act of 1964 but allows compensatory and punitive damages	• Same as Civil Rights Act of 1964

State Legislation

Most states within the US have EEO legislation that identifies additional forms of prohibited mistreatment. For example, the State of California has statutes that prohibit discrimination on the basis of marital status and sexual orientation and Michigan explicitly prohibits discrimination based on an individual's height or weight. As will be discussed in the next chapter, it is important that you identify any relevant State statutes where your organization operates and modify your mistreatment prevention and resolution system accordingly. One particularly helpful resource is provided by Cornell Law School (http://www.law.cornell.edu/topics/Table_Labor.htm), with links to the state statutes and governing agencies.

International EEO legislation

With the globalization of our workforce, it is not enough to consult relevant Federal, State, and local legislation. Your organization may have operations in other countries to which you send US citizens as expatriates, or your business may be based outside the US and you may employ host-country nationals, third-country nationals or, most likely, a combination. If so, your organization may need to adhere to another country's relevant mistreatment legislation in addition to adherence to US legislation in regards to treatment of your US employees. There are quite a few general similarities with regard to legislation. For example, countries in the European Union, as well as a number of others (e.g., Japan) have similar EEO legislation to the United States. However, some of these countries have protections for additional groups not covered by US legislation, outlawing, for example, discrimination based on geographic origin (UK), sexual orientation (EU), and social status (Japan). Also a number of countries have a "general just cause protection," so any type of mistreatment, not just mistreatment based on one of the protected categories we have mentioned, could be subject to legal action.[14] Such international EEO legislation should also be carefully consulted in designing a mistreatment prevention and resolution system in your organization.

Retaliation Issues

In addition to EEO legislation, there are other types of legislation and case law that are relevant to preventing or resolving mistreatment in the workplace. In particular, US whistle-blowing legislation (e.g., Whistleblower Protection Act, Sarbanes-Oxley Act) prohibits mistreatment in the form of retaliation for reporting unethical, unlawful, or other inappropriate organizational behavior. Most of the US EEO legislation (e.g., Title VII, ADEA) also prohibits retaliation against those who claim mistreatment under the legislation.

Labor Organizations

If a portion of your workforce is unionized, then the collective bargaining agreement between the union and management will define violations of that agreement as another form of mistreatment. For example, if the collective bargaining agreement specifies that seniority is to be used as a basis for determining who gets priority in vacation requests, then making a vacation request decision on the basis of, say, performance, would be a violation of the collective bargaining agreement and could be the basis for an employee's perception of mistreatment. In addition, the collective bargaining agreement typically identifies how the violation should be addressed (usually through a grievance system). Thus, if your workforce is unionized, you have additional types of mistreatment and may be restricted with respect to how you could address them.

It is important to note that not only would a collective bargaining agreement define violations as mistreatment, the collective bargaining agreement would also affect your discretion in designing and implementing a dispute resolution system to address such violations. That is, in a unionized setting the dispute resolution system would be negotiated as part of the collective bargaining agreement.

Contractual

More organizations are using carefully constructed arbitration clauses in their employment contracts. The arbitration clauses are usually signed before employment begins and are essentially waivers to employees using the court system to adjudicate a claim of illegal employment action. Instead the waiver stipulates the employee will have to use an alternative dispute resolution method, typically binding external arbitration. As noted by Alexander Colvin,[15] such arbitration clauses are being used by many large employers such as Citigroup, Discover Financial, and Circuit City. Colvin states "an estimated 15% to 20% of businesses now require employees to arbitrate disputes." Although there was originally some concern as to whether such arbitration clauses would hold up in court, when they have been challenged, the Federal courts have not struck down their use.[16]

Concluding Mistreatment – "I've Been Mistreated"

As previously indicated, our "mistreatment" term is an umbrella for a number of different types of mistreatment. But how do individuals reach a conclusion that they have been mistreated? We know from our experience and by our own empirical research that the process by which an employee concludes he or she has been mistreated is critical to understanding how to resolve this mistreatment and minimize its reoccurrence in the future. In this next section, the process of sense-making as it relates to mistreatment is explained.

The Sense-making Process

Sense-making is defined as "processes that people use to impose or derive structure or meaning when they experience complex, ambiguous, or stressful situations."[17] Typically people engage in sense-making by talking to others about the situation or by reflecting on what happened. Colloquially referred to as "processing," sense-making might include describing what happened to others and gauging their reactions, examining related policies, speaking with others who have experienced similar situations, or writing about it in a self-reflection exercise.

Case Scenario:
Making Sense of a Situation

Gwen has been an account manager at a large manufacturing firm. On Friday she asked her supervisor if she could leave two hours early that day to have extra time to get ready for her high school reunion. Her request was denied by her supervisor citing "this is our busy time" and then adding "it just doesn't seem all that important for you to have the time off." Gwen is frustrated and casually mentions the situation to her co-worker, Lisa, at lunch. Lisa and Gwen proceed to discuss the multiple examples of times that others have been allowed flexibility in their work schedules, noting that all of them are married and/or have children. Lisa then states, "I guess it's okay if you have a 'family' issue, but us single people aren't supposed to have lives." That evening, Gwen is rushed and ends up being late for her reunion.

Gwen thinks about the situation the rest of the weekend. She casually mentions what happened to a couple of her friends over coffee on Sunday. One friend asks Gwen if they have any policies at her company in regards to comp-time or flexible schedules. Another friend replies that she doesn't think it should matter, stating that if the manager has allowed employees to leave early before, then "that is the policy and it's unfair to not be consistent."

On Monday, Gwen decides to do some research on whether there are any informal or formal policies regarding time-off, comp-time, and the like at her company.

We know from research and practice that situations that lead to perceptions of mistreatment are often stressful to the individuals who experience them as well as ambiguous or complex. In response, employees usually engage in some sense-making before concluding they have been mistreated. This has several important implications for understanding mistreatment perceptions:

• Employees often do not *immediately* conclude they have been mistreated.
• Other organizational members, family members and friends will likely learn about and *influence* the individual's perception of mistreatment before the organization does.

With Whom Do Employees Typically Sense-make?

Employees may engage in sense-making about mistreatment with a wide variety of partners and groups. Parties to sense-making serve as "resource, reference, and social reinforcement."[18] Thus, employees may seek sense-making with people who have informational resources (e.g., external attorneys, human resource experts, psychologists, and individuals with understanding in the field). For reference sense-making, the employee may speak with coworkers or others who are familiar with the parties to the dispute or with people who have experienced similar situations. For social reinforcement, employees may seek out family members, coworkers, friends, clergy, and other supportive groups. Finally, an individual may engage in sense-making with himself or herself by reflecting on the incident or situation.

Good to Know:
Examples of Potential Partners to Sense-making

- Coworkers
- Family Members
- Friends and Neighbors
- Clergy
- Psychologists
- Union stewards or representatives

- Attorneys
- Human Resource Professionals
- Self

Does Sense-making Vary?

The existence, amount, and nature of the sense-making depend on the individual employee and the situation itself. Particularly ambiguous situations may result in a large amount of sense-making with a wide variety of parties because interpretations of the situation may vary considerably. On the other hand, complex situations may result in a high level of sense-making with fewer parties because of the investment required to be brought up to speed. Characteristics of the employee such as personality traits (e.g., extraversion) or prior experiences with similar situations will also play a role in how much sense-making he or she engages in before reaching a conclusion. In some scenarios, there might be little to no sense-making because of

---

Good to Know:
Some Factors Related to Little or No Sense-making

- *Situation is extreme or very clear.* For example, a manager says "I am not promoting you because you are a woman."
- *Employee's previous experience with a similar same situation.* For example, an employee has been similarly harassed before and quickly arrives at a conclusion of mistreatment.
- *Individual personality variables.* For example, individuals with high neuroticism may quickly arrive at a conclusion of mistreatment.

---

the characteristics of the situation, the employee's previous experiences, or the employee's personality.

Outcomes of the Sense-making Process

Influence of others

The people with whom an employee sense-makes will have a considerable amount of influence on the employee's perceptions. Research has shown that the opinions of others play a critical role in shaping someone's interpretation of a situation. For example, others may serve to reinforce or even enhance the employee's perception that he or she has been mistreated. Their initial reactions, particularly if they are strong, may heighten an individual's perception of mistreatment. Or others might share new information or remind the employee of other incidents that are consistent with mistreatment.

Others could serve to reduce an individual's initial perception of mistreatment by providing alternate ways to interpret the situation or explain how someone's motives might have been misunderstood. Others might offer an explanation for how someone's motives or "heart" could have been in the right place. This point is particularly relevant because it underscores the importance of others in the workplace in resolving and preventing mistreatment.

Case Scenario:
The Impact of Sense-making
on Conclusions of Mistreatment

Sue is a business administrator working for a government agency. Barry is Sue's new boss, recently transferred from another department at the same agency. A few days after Barry took on his new role, he met with Sue to discuss her job duties and his expectations. In the meeting, Barry asked Sue to prepare some complex analyses regarding the department's budget and said that he would need the information immediately so that he could get up to speed on the department's situation. Sue left the meeting feeling a bit overwhelmed with the assignment, but got to work and prepared the analyses for Barry. As the weeks continued, Sue found that Barry was giving her more and more

Continued

responsibilities but with little direction and supervision. She began to feel that Barry was taking advantage of her.

One evening Sue discussed the situation with her husband, Martin. She told him that though she enjoyed the added responsibility and challenge, she was concerned that Barry failed to recognize her hard work. She was worried that the added responsibility was because Barry felt she needed to "step it up," when in truth she had always been the highest performer in the workgroup. She was beginning to wonder whether Barry was planning to set her up for failure by adding responsibilities but not really supporting her. Sue added that she noticed other people in the department were not getting pushed by Barry like this and that he "may have it in for her." Martin said that she probably needed to give it some time and not jump to any conclusions about how Barry views her. He asked Sue what she knew about Barry's reputation as a manager and suggested she might try to get some insight on his style.

The next day, Sue dropped by her good friend Kristin's office, to get her thoughts. Kristin listened to Sue's story and then said "you are so off base!" Kristin went on to say that Sue was clearly a top performer and she bet Barry was leaning on her because he knew that. Kristin suggested Sue talk to Ryan who had worked with Barry on a project. Sue did this and learned from Ryan that Barry had no tolerance for low performers and that he had very high expectations for people he respected. His interpretation was that Barry clearly respected Sue otherwise he wouldn't trust her with such responsibility. He also informed her that Barry was a "hands off" manager, particularly when he knew the person was doing what needed to be done, and she should interpret Barry's treatment of her as positive.

Sue left the office that day feeling much better about the situation and concluded she was not being mistreated.

Conclusion of mistreatment (or not)

The ultimate outcome of the sense-making process is that the employee will conclude whether, and if so how, he or she has been mistreated. If the employee concludes mistreatment did occur, he or she will have some way of framing or characterizing the mistreatment, including what type of mistreatment is involved and who (or what) is at fault. For example, what started out as a description of the incident ("I didn't get the vacation days I requested") is now framed as discrimination ("I experienced discrimination because my manager is biased against people with children"). The employee will also have some perception of the intensity or seriousness of the mistreatment. This is an important factor in how or whether the employee will pursue addressing the mistreatment as well as in how the employee will respond behaviorally, psychologically, and physiologically to the mistreatment.

Subsequent effects
Another important consequence of sense-making is that the others involved in an individual's sense-making will also be affected by learning about the incident or situation. Coworkers' perceptions of others in the organization (e.g., manager, other coworkers) could be altered through the discussions about the situation. Similarly, the coworkers' perceptions of the employee could change. Such knowledge and/or discussion could contribute to a culture of mistrust or hostility within the organization. Coworkers may also engage in their own sense-making process whereby they begin to consider (or reconsider) situations that they were involved in personally. The key point is that any one incident is likely to have implications for how other and future situations are interpreted and perceived by those involved in the sense-making process.

Good to Know:
Key Points

- Mistreatment in the workplace can take many forms including inequitable treatment, unfair processes or policies, incivility, bullying, and organizational wrongdoing (e.g., discrimination, retaliation).
- Some forms of mistreatment are expressly prohibited by legislation or contractual agreement.

- Through the sense-making process, an employee concludes whether he or she has been mistreated.
- The existence, amount, and nature of the sense-making depend on the individual employee and the situation.

Chapter 3

Workplace Scanning for Potential, Nascent, and Existent Mistreatment Issues

This chapter discusses how you can be proactive in heading off or attenuating developing issues through scanning your organizational environment for problem areas. Scanning is the *careful, systematic review of information* about mistreatment issues in the organization. These mistreatment issues may be in various levels of development. That is, they might be:

- *Potential mistreatment issues*: Something has the potential of resulting in perceptions of mistreatment (e.g., an upcoming merit pay decision)
- *Nascent mistreatment issues*: Perceptions of mistreatment have just started to develop (e.g., employees have questioned the rationale of a new policy or expressed frustration about it).
- *Existent mistreatment issues*: Perceptions of mistreatment have already developed, but are not yet pervasive (e.g., an employee feels verbally abused by a manager, and is trying to make sense of the situation).

Regardless of the level of development, the objective of scanning is to detect and head off issues before they develop into full-scale mistreatment or escalate into more substantive problems. This is like finding a potential problem before it becomes a problem or finding a smaller problem early. It doesn't mean "looking for trouble," but rather keeping an ear attuned to potential issues so preventive actions can be taken or the problem can be resolved earlier rather than later.

What Are the Potential Sources of Information for Scanning?

How do you know about potential, nascent, or existent mistreatment issues in your organization? In order to identify such issues, the scanning process must consist of a *careful, systematic review of information from a wide range of voice*. According to Albert Hirschman's[1] economic model (the Exit, Voice, Loyalty Model), as applied to the employment context, *voice is any way by which an employee might provide input at work, or signal/communicate that there is a problem or potential problem at work*. This can range from an off-hand remark regarding an incident to an employee filing a lawsuit against the organization. At first blush, some voice mechanisms, such as problem-solving teams or staff meetings, may not appear to be voice mechanisms. But if they involve employees providing input about how things are conducted in the organization, then they would be considered as such. You may have several institutionalized voice mechanisms in your organization, including a dispute resolution system (discussed in fuller detail in Chapters 5–8).

Examples:
Institutionalized Voice Mechanisms in Organizations

- Participation on taskforces and employee-management committees
- Problem-solving teams
- Soliciting input during staff meetings
- Suggestions made to a suggestion box
- Climate surveys
- Focus groups or "stay" interviews
- Exit surveys
- Use of an open-door policy
- Use of a multi-step appeal process
- Use of an ethics hot-line

Institutionalized Proactive Sources

Some institutionalized voice mechanisms are proactive in that they are more likely to identify *potential mistreatment issues* or *nascent mistreatment issues*. Thus such methods, by their nature and timing, could serve to prevent mistreatment altogether or address developing perceptions of mistreatment early, preventing them from developing into larger problems. These sources would include processes or policies that allow (or require) employee participation or input such as those described below.

Examples:
Proactive Sources

- *Taskforces.* Employees participating in a small group that is charged with completing a particular project (e.g., revising a merit pay system) would be able to provide input about potential mistreatment issues, ultimately changing the direction of the decision. For example, a production employee might describe how changing a piece-rate system would be perceived by his or her coworkers. A careful review or response to such feedback can prevent mistreatment from occurring.
- *Suggestion Box.* A suggestion box allows employees to provide (typically anonymous) input about an issue. Careful review of feedback provided through a suggestion box can serve as a catalyst for preventing a developing mistreatment issue from becoming a substantive problem.
- *Climate Surveys.* Surveys can be used to monitor employee attitudes and perceptions. Systematic, ongoing administration of climate surveys (e.g., annually) allows an organization to monitor trends, thus serving as a signal to intervene before an issue escalates.

Institutionalized Reactive Sources

Other institutionalized voice mechanisms such as multi-step appeal processes (e.g., grievance procedure) are designed to provide resolution for mistreatment, but in the process of doing so serve to uncover existing mistreatment problems (which may or may not be the focus of the mistreatment issue at hand). As will be described in more detail in Chapter 8, reviewing or scanning these sources and responding to this information can serve to minimize the potential impact of an existent mistreatment issue in your organization.

Non-Institutionalized Sources

Employees may also voice or communicate problems in ways that are not necessarily institutionalized by your organization. In other words, employees may come up with their own ways to communicate a problem.

Examples:
Non-Institutionalized Voice Mechanisms

- Anonymous comments written on a posted notice
- Off-hand remarks made about a co-worker or other member of the organization
- Comments made to organizational outsiders (e.g., friends, family)
- Behavioral withdrawal (e.g., decreased job performance)
- Exit from the organization

These non-institutionalized approaches can vary in terms of utility to you but are often not considered to be desirable forms of voice. For example, adverse performance-related withdrawal is potentially of great detriment and cost to your organization. And, while an employee venting to an organizational outsider (or even insider) may seem relatively harmless, such approaches do not ensure that the organization learns of the issue that needs to be addressed and may also have deleterious effects such as diminishing the organization's reputation as an employer or generating discontent among others in the workgroup.

On the other hand, while scanning non-institutionalized voice mechanisms is arguably more challenging, it can yield some valuable information. The key is to maintain a finger on the pulse of the organization by watching for signals such as off-hand comments, informal or unsolicited feedback, and behavioral withdrawal among employees and to use this information to your organization's advantage. Tools can also be developed for employees (perhaps even non-employees) to provide information anonymously and unsolicited via the company intranet (or internet). In a sense, non-institutionalized mechanisms for voicing such as off-handed comments can become institutionalized.

Case Scenario:
The Value of Attending to Non-Institutionalized Sources

A training instructor for a geographically dispersed insurance company was responsible for delivering training in a number of different locations. One day the trainer called into the Human Resources office at headquarters to ask that someone post a sign in the headquarters training room stating that the training session would be cancelled due to illness. This was the first time he had "called in sick" that year. A sign was placed in the training room. However, the following week an HR professional noticed, while setting up the training room for a different trainer, that several people had written on the posted canceled class announcement the words "always," "as usual," and "gee, what a surprise." Upon further investigation, it was found that the trainer had missed several previous training sessions (in other locations) but had not reported it to HR so that his sick days would not be charged. The trainees (all entry-level employees) were frustrated because they felt unprepared for their insurance certification exam and thought it was not fair that they had not been given the proper training as had been promised to them. Although anonymous writing on a posted sign is not an institutionalized scanning source, it served as a valuable source of information and allowed the HR department to address the growing resentment by making a staffing change and adding make-up training sessions.

How Do You Evaluate Your Scanning Sources?

One important consideration is whether your institutionalized sources will provide you with the information you need for scanning.

Our experience has taught us that there are several important criteria to consider in evaluating your current scanning sources.

Tips:
Criteria for Evaluating Scanning Sources

- Do you offer a variety of available mechanisms?
- Does at least one of the voice mechanisms allow for anonymous input?
- Do employees believe their input will be heard and considered?
- Are policies such as employee participation programs mere rhetoric; not put into practice?

Variety Criterion

Offering a variety of proactive and reactive mechanisms allows you to identify potential, nascent, and existent mistreatment while accommodating both the differences in individuals' preferences for how to voice and the contextual factors involved in any one situation. For example, with respect to reactive voice mechanisms, personal characteristics such as an individual's conflict style and the nature of the relationship with the other involved party are likely to influence his or her preferred approaches to voicing. In addition, the most effective source is likely to vary depending on the nature of the issue and the level of development. Further, by offering more and different sources, you are simply more likely to capture the information you need about mistreatment in your organization.

Anonymity Criterion

Employees need to feel comfortable providing candid and honest information, with no fear of reprisal. This may be particularly important for identifying potential or nascent issues because an individual may still be sense-making and may not be confident that mistreatment has occurred (or is about to occur). It is thus important to provide at least one anonymous outlet to voice issues. Anonymous sources are particularly critical for uncovering very sensitive information.

Input Heard and Considered Criterion

Another important determinant of whether your scanning sources are appropriate centers on whether employees believe that the scanning sources are effective and viable options for raising or addressing issues. If, for example, employees perceive that their voice is not being heard (that it is falling on "deaf ears"[2]) or their perspectives or concerns are not taken into consideration, they will be unmotivated to utilize voice mechanisms. Employees who do not believe anything will change will be unlikely, for example, to provide suggestions or honest assessments of a situation. Perhaps even more deleterious is if employees believe they will be "punished" for voicing (e.g., labeled as troublemakers), which is not uncommon when the person they might be speaking out about is in a power position (e.g., a supervisor) or seen as a particularly valuable or talented employee. In sum, the process needs to be relatively easy for employees to use and employees should believe their voice will be heard and considered.

Policies Put into Practice Criterion

You may say (and believe) that employees are afforded opportunities to voice issues and participate in decision-making within your organization, but do employees actually take advantage of such opportunities? If not, there may be a disconnect between an organization's *intended* policies and the *actual* programs or processes that are put into practice. With large corporations, in particular, there is always the challenge of ensuring intended policies are actually enacted.

In our experience, a key challenge in implementing organization-level policies to the staff is the immediate supervisor. Though a manager may make a decision not to enact an organizational policy, perhaps because he or she does not agree with its premise, there is also evidence that line managers may simply be unaware of the policy themselves. This supports the importance of understanding whether policies aimed at scanning are put into practice as intended – and if not, why not. It is only the enacted policies (regardless of what is in the policy/personnel manual) that can be utilized by employees and be of value to your organization.

How Can You Tell Whether Your System Meets These Criteria?

We have identified several important criteria that your scanning sources should fulfill, but the ultimate question is how do you know whether your system actually meets them? There are several ways you can evaluate the situation.

- One clear signal is the *usage rate* of various mechanisms. That is, what percentage of your employees are offering suggestions, participating in task force discussion, or completing the climate survey? Analyzing trends over time allows you to monitor how usage is improving (or declining) perhaps due to an intervention (e.g., training, organizational change effort). Though anonymity is important, as previously discussed, tracking usage rates by department or business unit levels provides insight on trouble areas within the larger organization.
- Are occurrences of mistreatment surfacing without prior indication? That is, is your organization "taken by surprise" by issues brought to your formal dispute resolution system or even by external litigation? If so, this would also suggest your scanning sources are not effective in identifying potential or nascent issues. You can evaluate where the breakdown is occurring either through the use of additional anonymous methods or through follow-up with individuals involved in incidents that surfaced later rather than sooner.
- Is there a change in personnel variables (e.g., turnover, absences) over time? Tracking such information over time is quite valuable in offering insight on patterns of changes in the workplace. Deteriorations in employee attitudes or increased rate of turnover may signal problems. Again, tracking this data at the department or business unit level provides a clearer understanding of trouble spots within your organization.
- Assessing employee perceptions of the voice mechanisms may be useful (see Chapter 8). Surveying employees, most likely through anonymous surveys, on their perceptions, intended use, and suggestions provides you with direct feedback on the system.

Develop a System to Systematically Review/Audit Information

The objective of scanning is not simply to gather information, but to head off issues. It is thus important to incorporate a purposeful and systematic review or audit of the information acquired through your scanning sources. Such a review can take two forms. A *periodic review* involves analyzing the information at a planned time, perhaps quarterly or annually. During the planned review, issues regarding the scanning system, individual mechanisms, and specific issues of mistreatment (or potential mistreatment) would be examined. We have found that periodic reviews, unfortunately, are often not top priorities in organizations. However, to maximize the chance of heading off potential or nascent mistreatment issues, audits need to be conducted regularly, even during times of apparently "smooth sailing." Our experience has shown that those organizations that do make periodic reviews a top priority enjoy significant returns on their investment. For example, one company we have worked with conducts a quarterly review of its voice mechanisms. This company uses several sources including an anonymous electronic voice mechanism and a yearly climate survey. During one quarterly review, the auditors noticed a number of anonymous comments about the unfair pay and benefits offered by the company, but they were all made in reference, or relative to a local competitor. The climate survey had recently been conducted, and there was lower compensation satisfaction for one general job category. Upon further exploration, the company learned that the competitor had recently raised its starting pay (and benefits) in an effort to lure these hard-to-hire employees away. The company was able to act quickly and prevent further compensation dissatisfaction and turnover.

Beyond the planned period review, a systematic review should occur on an *as needed* basis. What would trigger such a review? Certainly, significant signals such as a lawsuit, claim of harassment, or unionization campaign would warrant a review. Other changes within the organization such as a new leadership, merger with (or acquisition of) another firm, or strategic refocus would be good times to reassess information regarding developing or potential issues and trouble spots. Such events are likely to bring uncertainty and adjustments to the workplace and thus would be a good time for you to investigate what employees are experiencing and where efforts may be needed to head off problems.

Foster a Voice-Supportive Culture

If you can develop a culture where voice is embraced, then it is more likely issues will be expressed and addressed early on before they develop into substantive problems. What would such a culture look like?

Good to Know: Voice-Supportive Culture	
Individuals must feel free to:	Without:
• voice their concerns • provide input and information • utilize work systems aimed at employee involvement and participative decision-making	• concerns about being unheard • confidentiality being betrayed • feeling judged, contentious, prejudiced, or disrespected • fear of reprisal

The criteria discussed earlier regarding multiple scanning mechanisms and the nature of these mechanisms (e.g., allowing for anonymity, perceived as effective) are critical elements of such a culture. Assurances of confidentiality must be rigorously protected to maintain trust and to enhance a supportive voice culture. But, more generally, the workplace culture must be one of respect, tolerance, cooperation, and collaboration. This is consistent with the notion of an open work environment which helps to foster a culture where ideas are expressed freely and concerns addressed sooner rather than later.[3] Opportunities for proactive voice through the implementation of problem-solving teams, employee participation in decision-making, labor–management committees, and the like are typically consistent with and reinforcing of a workplace culture aimed at preventing (as well as resolving) mistreatment. If employees have a genuine opportunity to influence decisions and voice concerns before final action is taken, this helps ensure potentially problematic issues come to light.[4] PSS World Medical is one example of a company which appears to be experiencing benefits from making a voice-supportive culture a priority. PSS World Medical's culture is characterized as very open and encouraging of questions and input. In fact, the CEO and other officers have been known to "carry $2 bills with them and give them out to anyone who asks a question."[5] In addition, one of PSS World Medical's values is "ALWAYS communicate without fear of retribution."[6]

Good to Know:
Key Points

- Scanning your organization's voice mechanisms will allow you to head off potential, nascent, and existent mistreatment issues.
- It is important to have a broad range of scanning sources including at least one that allows anonymity.
- Your scanning sources should be carefully examined and audited to ensure they are providing the information you need, and your employees are using them to signal problems as they occur.

- The information gleaned from your scanning sources should be examined both periodically and as needed.
- Fostering a voice-supportive culture is critical to being able to prevent or catch mistreatment early through the use of scanning.

Chapter 4

Preventing Mistreatment through Workplace Practices

Preventing mistreatment is in a way like minimizing your risk of a health problem. There may be a number of things you can do to minimize your risk of contracting a certain disease, such as eating (or avoiding) certain foods, physical activity, avoiding toxins, and the like. Similarly, there may be certain steps you can take to "catch a disease early," and, as a result, be able to use less invasive methods for its treatment.

In this chapter, we discuss several workplace practices which can serve to prevent mistreatment in your organization including:

- Developing recruitment and selection systems which help to prevent or minimize mistreatment
- Developing and implementing training systems which serve to prevent or minimize mistreatment
- Examining and revising your reward structures so that mistreatment is not rewarded
- Developing managers so that they have the skills to prevent or minimize mistreatment
- Using disciplinary actions, including terminations, appropriately, so that chronic mistreatment is avoided

Before continuing with this discussion, it is important to point out the parameters of mistreatment prevention.

Good to Know:
A Word of Caution About Mistreatment Prevention

- *Nothing is fail-proof.* These methods *are by no means fail-proof.* You can certainly minimize your organization's risk, and you can find and address smaller problems before they become bigger, but you will not eliminate all perceptions of mistreatment.
- *Some level of disagreement is good.* As noted earlier, research has clearly demonstrated that conflict does have its benefits. In particular, a certain level of disagreement (e.g., over how to complete a task) is advantageous to an organization. In your efforts to minimize mistreatment, your organization should be careful not to squelch healthy disagreements.

Developing Recruitment and Selection Systems to Help Prevent Mistreatment

An obvious time to try to head off potential mistreatment is prior to employees even joining the organization. Through your employee recruitment and selection practices, you can try to establish expectations regarding interpersonal interaction in the workplace and perhaps even predict and select out individuals who are likely instigators of mistreatment.

Set Expectations for Interpersonal Treatment

If you want to establish and maintain a culture in your organization that serves to minimize mistreatment, the *expectations of interpersonal treatment* in the workplace need to be communicated to potential employees. There are a number of ways to approach this.

- *Include information about these expectations in the recruitment message.* That is, if you expect employees to be considerate and respectful of others and to work out differences when they occur, then explain the work culture in the job announcement. As examples, companies such as Shell Oil, Halliburton, and Lockheed

Martin emphasize interpersonal treatment (such as respect) as core organizational values in their recruiting material.

- *Examine how the potential employee is treated during the recruitment process.* All the verbiage in the world will not work if you don't "walk the talk" during the recruitment process. Research has shown that applicant experiences during the recruitment and selection process have an important effect on applicant perceptions of the organization including fairness perceptions.[1] The way potential employees are treated during recruitment will shape their expectations of how they will be treated as employees and how they should treat others in your organization. Many companies fall short in this area, acting rudely or arrogantly as well as conveying disrespect by being unprepared, uninterested, or uninformed during the recruitment process.[2] Other companies we have worked with demonstrate respect for applicants by making interview arrangements which work best for the applicant, giving them personal "down time" in between a busy interview schedule, and providing them with opportunities to gather candid, full information about the organization by speaking directly with employees who are not a part of the formal recruitment process.

- *Make priorities known throughout the selection process.* Expectations regarding interpersonal treatment at your organization can be tied in with the message you send about your culture. The objective is to communicate to potential employees that respect at your organization is critical. This can be beneficial in at least two general ways.

  - *Promote self-selection in and out of your organization by providing realism on the culture and expectations.* Prior research on realistic job previews (RJPs) demonstrates that applicants who do not "fit" with or like what they hear about the organization will remove themselves from the selection process. Conversely, by promoting good interpersonal treatment through your selection process, you will encourage individuals attracted to such a culture to remain interested in employment opportunities.

  - *Establish expectations to help define behaviors from the beginning.* Research has discussed this as an employee's *psychological contract*, or his or her beliefs about the terms and conditions of the exchange relationship between him or herself and the organization.[3] Providing a clear message about how employees at your organization are treated and how they are to treat others helps to define the psychological contract regarding respect versus mistreatment in the workplace.

How to Screen Out Potential Problem Employees

There are a number of excellent resources on employee selection,[4] and a discussion of what is known about how best to select employees is beyond the scope of this book. However, it is important to identify how organizational selection practices can serve to minimize or even prevent mistreatment in the workplace. In this section we discuss, in general terms, how some selection tools can be used for these purposes. Before implementing these tools, we recommend you consult additional literature.

Personnel selection is the process of making decisions on who to employ and who not to employ within your organization. The goal is to predict who will be effective, and the most effective, in performing the job. The process involves determining the predictors of future job performance (e.g., computer skills, verbal ability) and then measuring and assessing those criteria for each applicant, ultimately making a decision on whom to hire (and whom not). Through this process, you can take steps to identify where potential problem employees may exist.

Selection criteria
The first step to developing the appropriate selection criteria is to perform a rigorous job analysis. Through the job analysis, you will obtain detailed information about what is required to carry out the job. As we know from the extant practice and research literature on employee selection, there are a variety of general characteristics that you may want to assess and use as the basis for selection decisions including such content areas as job knowledge and abilities.

Clearly, the technical capability to do the job is critical. But also important are interpersonal and communication skills, and the ability to work well with others even under stressful circumstances. In our experience, the presence or absence of such skills and abilities is a particularly useful predictor of whether an individual is likely to mistreat others at work or is likely to be able (or willing) to address mistreatment should it occur. Assessing personality traits from the Five Factor Model,[5] such as agreeableness, conscientiousness, and emotional stability, may also be informative, though validation studies showing the relationship between such assessment and job performance are needed to assess the appropriateness of use for a particular context.

Selection methods
The research literature is replete with evidence that "past behavior is the best predictor of future behavior."[6] To that end, it would be helpful to identify individuals who have previously mistreated others at work. Though no organization has perfected the process, organizations such as Southwest, Google, IDEO, and Jetblue Airlines are famous for emphasizing "human qualities" and screening out potential problems through the hiring process. There are several tools that such organizations use for this purpose and that you might use as well. They include:

- *Behavioral interviewing.* This structured interview technique requires applicants to describe, in detail, how they behaved in the past in a certain type of situation.[7] The questions are generated via a critical incident technique in which subject matter experts (often job incumbents) describe real situations and work behaviors that have occurred in that organization. These critical incidents are then used to create interview questions (see example below). Empirical research has demonstrated this technique is quite effective in predicting which applicants will perform well on the job.[8] Assuming job-relatedness, you could use this technique to uncover how an applicant has behaved in situations that may raise mistreatment issues.

  There are several benefits of using this approach. First, from a validity perspective, how an individual behaved in the past is a good predictor of how they would behave in similar situations in your organization. Second, such questions may communicate to potential employees the importance placed on interpersonal treatment in your organization. It is always wise to involve multiple interviewers in the process, including those who will work with the individual, in order to get the most complete "picture" of the applicant.

Example:
Behavioral Interviewing

- *Critical incident*: Sales representatives described the following situation that occurred with a sales manager in their organization. One of the sales representatives had a child who suffered a serious medical emergency. The sales representative asked the manager if he could temporarily cut back some of the travel responsibilities so that he could stay close to his child. The manager replied on-the-spot "either work or quit, your family is not our concern."
- *Interview question*: Describe a situation in the past where you, as a manager, were asked to make an accommodation for a personal need of one of your employees. How did you make your decision and how did you convey your decision to the employee?

- *Reference checks.* Another way to measure how someone behaved in the past is to ask those who had the opportunity to observe that applicant in the work context. Typically this is done through reference checks in which the potential employer contacts a previous employer as well as other contacts and specifically inquires about the applicant's behavior. Reference checks are considered a selection measure, so you should be careful to follow the same steps you would follow with other devices (i.e., job analysis, structured job-related questions, trained reference takers, documentation, written permission from applicants). Unfortunately, the use of this approach is problematic, at best. Early empirical evidence shows a weak relationship between information from a reference check and employee job performance, yet more recent evidence suggests that reference checks can be improved through structuring the questions asked and the process.[9] However, organizations have traditionally been hesitant to give information that might be particularly useful to another employer (e.g., did this individual mistreat others?) out of fear of libel or slander claims. This fear may be generally unfounded, as most states provide protection to reference givers so long as any information (both positive and negative) provided is factual and material to the applicant's fitness for employment.

- *Assessment centers.* Another valuable selection device for these purposes might be the assessment center technique. Assessment centers are typically conducted over multiple (2–3) days, use multiple exercises (e.g., in-basket, leaderless group discussions, role plays) with multiple raters. Given the expense, assessment centers are most often used to select or promote managers. Although there is still debate, in practice and research, on what is actually measured in assessment centers, there is compelling evidence that assessment centers predict job performance. Observing how potential managers interact with others under stressful circumstances would be a good indication of the likelihood that their behavior would create perceptions of mistreatment in the workplace.

- *Integrity testing.* Also referred to as honesty tests, integrity tests involve the formal assessment of an applicant's attitudes and moral character. Though the major justification for using such tests is to determine which applicants are most likely to steal from the company, such tests may also offer more general insight on an individual's tendency to engage in undesirable workplace behavior related to interpersonal mistreatment (e.g., low conscientiousness, unsociability). There are a variety of integrity tests commercially available,[10] though of course, the validity of any one test in predicting dysfunctional work behavior should be carefully examined given concerns about misclassifying an honest applicant as dishonest (and vice versa).

- *Promotion decisions.* A special selection case is deciding who to promote to supervisory or managerial positions. All too often individuals are promoted to team leader, supervisor, or manager based on their technical performance in their current jobs, with little attention to how they might interact with others at work. Given the importance of interpersonal communication skills to performance in these jobs, a careful examination of these skills would be quite beneficial. Such an examination might include carefully reviewing previous evaluations that measure those aspects of performance as well as purposely soliciting feedback via coworkers, clients, etc. (i.e., a 360 degree performance appraisal). Assessment centers, discussed previously, are another viable approach to evaluating the management or leadership potential of an employee.

When Selecting for "Mistreatment" Matters Most

There are some roles in your organization for which it is particularly critical that the individuals filling those roles are well equipped to minimize or prevent mistreatment. These include the following:

- *Managers/Supervisors/Team Leaders:* These individuals are critical for two reasons. First, they make a number of decisions (e.g., scheduling, pay, task assignment) that could potentially be perceived as the basis for mistreatment. Second, they are often the first person to whom an individual might signal mistreatment. Their ability to resolve the mistreatment early on and appropriately has important implications for employee reactions to mistreatment and future behaviors.
- *Human Resources/Dispute Resolution Administrators:* These individuals are tasked with the responsibility of addressing mistreatment (e.g., answering questions about policy, providing guidance for resolution) and often serve as facilitators in dealing with mistreatment if it has occurred. Having individuals in these positions who actually exacerbate or initiate mistreatment could be particularly problematic. This was a particular problem in one company we worked with, as illustrated in the example below.

Case Scenario:
When Selection Matters Most

A smaller organization in the food industry had several policies and procedures related to addressing mistreatment in the workplace. In all the relevant policies and procedures the employees were to speak with the Human Resource Director if the employee felt he or she had been mistreated in any way.

After two years of employment, one of the younger professionals, "Andrew," started to experience what he considered to be sexual harassment. Another employee, "Lauren," had started to "go out of her way" to touch him when he worked at his desk, blocked his passage when he moved in the hallway and initiated multiple, explicit conversations about sex. Unfortunately, Lauren was the Human Resource Director at the organization. Unsure of who to talk to, Andrew sought the advice of a number of people outside the organization, including other HR professionals, an attorney, and his MBA professor. Andrew seriously considered quitting his job because he was not sure how his complaint would be received in the organization. Eventually Andrew spoke directly to the owner and the situation was resolved. However, the situation could have been resolved much more quickly (and less publicly) if the Human Resource Director position had been staffed by someone else.

• *Employees Working Primarily in a Team Setting:* Companies have begun to recognize that technical skills, experience, and job knowledge are not enough to ensure effectiveness particularly when jobs require extensive interdependence and interpersonal interactions among individuals. Selecting individuals who will "fit" the workgroup thus becomes a critical element to help ensure positive working relationships and reduce the likelihood of interpersonal mistreatment. This suggests that the workgroup should be involved in selecting their future team/group members. At a recent executive development class in the Houston, Texas area, over half of the participants indicated involving the employees they supervise in the selection process of new employees. The premise is that if an individual will be expected to work closely with someone, he/she should have input on the selection decision.

Developing and Implementing Training Systems to Help Prevent Mistreatment

When it comes to employees' skills and abilities, you have to face the "buy or make" decision. Selection focuses on the buying approach, where you bring individuals into the organization who already possess (presumably) the capability to do the job. Training is about making (that is, developing) the skills among your employees. While it may be possible, and it is clearly valuable, to focus on preventing future mistreatment issues when making hiring decisions, training is also useful to head off issues before they develop into mistreatment or escalate into more substantive problems. In this section we identify three major ways you might use training to prevent, minimize, or address mistreatment effectively:

- Orienting and socializing newcomers
- Training on appropriate/inappropriate workplace conduct
- Training to address mistreatment

Orienting and Socializing Newcomers

The first opportunity for training employees to prevent mistreatment is during the orientation, or on-boarding, program. On-boarding typically occurs during the employees' first few days on the job, thus offering an early opportunity to establish expectations among your new hires. This orientation is designed to prepare employees to perform the job, learn about the organization's values and policies, and establish work relationships.

Tips:
Information to Include During On-Boarding

- Expectations about how employees will treat one another, and clients, at work.
- Information on departmental and corporate values
- Workplace policies regarding employment decisions (e.g., promotions, pay determination)
- Mechanisms and resources for resolving differences and/or addressing mistreatment
- The role of a mentor

Communicate expectations
This is the time to communicate expectations regarding interpersonal treatment of coworkers. Even if such information was conveyed through the recruitment and staffing processes, it is useful to reinforce and expand on these expectations. Further, it is likely that some level of detail regarding workplace policies and expectations was not discussed with job applicants and thus needs to be established upon organizational entry.

Communicate departmental and corporate values
On-boarding is an ideal time to explain your values. To the extent these values tie in with mistreatment, this would also be an appropriate time to explain, with concrete examples, how your corporate values are "put into action." For example, if one of your core values is "respect" then you might explain what that means for the employment context.

Case Scenario:
Communicating Values

A bank in the Midwest takes value socialization of newcomers very seriously. Every new hire participates in a four-hour on-boarding process focused specifically on organizational norms and values (e.g., valuing diversity, respect for colleagues). The information is disseminated via manuals, discussions with human resources and supervisors, and videos. Following this general organizational on-boarding process, information specific to the workgroup and department is communicated to the new hire so as to reinforce the alignment between workgroup, departmental and organizational values. The new hire is also matched up with a "buddy" (similar to a mentor) who is available to answer additional questions and promote socialization informally during the first few weeks of employment.

Explain processes used to make employment decisions
As we know from the research on interactional justice (i.e., the importance of being treated with dignity and respect), being provided with information on why procedures are used and how decisions are made heightens perceptions of fairness. Thus, a description of how performance is evaluated, raises are determined, and promotions are made would be valuable in preventing perceptions of mistreatment. This information should also be available in a personnel manual and/or on the company intranet to provide readily accessible information should employees have a question or an issue arise that needs clarification.

Describe and explain mechanisms and resources for resolving differences and/or addressing mistreatment

In our experience, employees are not always aware of the resources and mechanisms that their organization has available for preventing and/or addressing mistreatment. Obviously, if employees are unaware of such tools, it is unlikely they would serve their original purpose. The on-boarding process is a critical time to describe the available dispute resolution options and convey that your organization supports their use.

Mentoring

A common element of many organizations' on-boarding process is use of a mentoring program. Mentoring is "a relationship between two individuals, usually a senior and junior employee, whereby the senior employee takes the junior employee 'under his or her wing' to teach the junior employee about his or her job, introduce the junior employee to contacts, orient the employee to the industry and organization, and address social and personal issues that may arise on the job."[11] Given this role, mentors are in a good position to reinforce expectations to organizational newcomers but also to ensure that an employee has someone to go to other than the supervisor should a situation arise. This point is particularly important if a mistreatment incident involves the supervisor. The mentor can offer a valuable perspective and sounding board during the sense-making process and can also provide information about resources.

Tips:
Use of Mentoring in Preventing Mistreatment

- Provide support to new employee
- Reinforce expectations
- Be a source for sense-making or a resource for employee should a problem arise

---

People who serve as mentors need to be carefully selected to ensure that they have strong interpersonal and communication skills and are themselves unlikely to exacerbate or initiate mistreatment. Also important is that the individuals involved in the mentoring relationship are compatible. Some consideration of personality types and commitment to the program, for example, may help ensure that the protégé will feel comfortable utilizing the mentor as a resource and that the mentor is responsive to issues raised by the protégé.

Case Scenario:
An Ineffective Mentoring Relationship

As part of a government agency's formal mentoring program for individuals from underrepresented groups, Jose was assigned Robin as a mentor to help him get adjusted in his new work role and serve as a support system for any challenges he faced.

After two weeks on the job, Jose began to feel overwhelmed by his work responsibilities and a bit disconnected from his work group. Jose felt his manager was not supportive of him and that, in fact, his manager seemed to be giving him tasks that were too advanced for him as a brand new employee. He sent an email to Robin asking if they could get together to talk so that he could get her advice on strategies for tackling the workload and work relationships. Robin quickly responded with an email message that she would get back to Jose after completing a large project due later that month. Privately, Robin couldn't understand what problems Jose could have already and felt he was probably a "squeaky wheel." When the two finally did get together two weeks after the initial email from Jose, they found the conversation awkward and unproductive. Robin had no experience with the issues Jose was facing and thus had little to offer in terms of advice. In the following weeks, Jose continued to feel overwhelmed and disconnected, but did not approach his mentor again perceiving it was of little value. Robin assumed that Jose's issues had been resolved. Jose quit his job three months later.

Training on Appropriate/Inappropriate Workplace Conduct

As with employee selection, there are a number of excellent resources on the training of employees,[12] and a discussion of what we know about how to design and implement training programs is beyond the scope of this book. However, it is important to identify how training can serve to minimize or even prevent mistreatment in the workplace. In this section we discuss, in general terms, how training programs can be used for these purposes. Before implementing these tools, we recommend you consult additional literature.

Needs assessment

As with any training program, instructional design should be used to develop training systematically to meet the specific needs of your organization. This process begins with a needs assessment. Needs assessment is the process of determining if and where training is necessary[13] and involves three types of analysis.

- *Organizational analysis*: where training is needed, whether there are resources available, and whether there is support by managers and other constituents for the training activities.
- *Task analysis*: identifying the important tasks and competencies that need to be emphasized in the training.
- *Person analysis:* determining whether deficiencies are due to lack of competency or other factors (e.g., motivation, work design), who needs training, and whether employees are ready for training.

After conducting such an assessment you may determine that a particular kind of training is needed periodically for all employees to ensure awareness and understanding of appropriate and inappropriate workplace conduct. Or, you may reach the conclusion that certain employees, such as employees recently promoted to supervisory or team leader roles or transferred or promoted to positions where issues related to workplace mistreatment are critical (e.g., HR roles, customer contact), need to complete a particular training program once. Outside the systematic needs assessment process, something may prompt an organization to become aware that there is a training need.

Good to Know:
There May Be a Training Need When . . .

- Use of your dispute resolution system is markedly high or on the rise
- Your organization faces a lawsuit

- Institutionalized scanning sources reveal a potential issue
- Your organization has recently undergone or is about to undergo a signifi-cant change (e.g., imple-ment work teams, change in leadership)
- There has been a recent influx of new employees (or supervisors/managers)

- There is a general sense of discontent among your workforce
- There is a high level or rise in turnover or absenteeism
- Or . . . you simply want to be proactive in preventing mistreatment!

Content areas
Beyond the early days of employment, training can be an effective tool for developing and reinforcing employees' knowledge and skills with regard to workplace conduct. Developing such skills and knowledge in your employees can serve to prevent some forms of mistreatment from occurring or could enable employees to address mistreatment early on. Although it may be desirable to do so, it may not be realistic to only hire employees who have, for example, superb interpersonal and communication skills. Yet, through training programs you have the opportunity to further develop these skills in your workforce. In the table below we describe several training content areas that could be beneficial in preventing or resolving mistreatment issues.

Tips:
Training Content Areas to Consider

- Communication skills (including listening)
- Harassment (what it is and policies surrounding it)
- Interpersonal training in workgroups
- Understanding fairness and perspective taking
- Administration of policies
- Customer service
- Diversity (e.g., race, gender, values, generational, cultural)

Please note that you should be extremely cautious in implementing a diversity training program. Some of the earlier diversity training efforts were very problematic and "failed because of their focus on awareness, understanding, and appreciating differences . . . and created more divisiveness and disruption than existed before."[14] For example, some training sessions resulted in harassment and discrimination claims because of what participants experienced in the process of others sharing common biases and stereotypes. Instead, we know from evidence-based practice that when focusing on such a sensitive area as diversity, you should focus on changing behaviors in the workplace, rather than focusing on underlying attitudes.

Training methods
Once the need for training is identified and the content of the training determined, the question then becomes how such training should be offered. There are a variety of training methods available. The key is to deliver the training based on the objectives.

Tips:
Training Methods to Facilitate Appropriate Workplace Conduct

- Behavior modeling
- Role playing
- Simulations
- Computerized instruction
- Videos
- Business games/Case studies

We recommend the use of training utilizing hands-on methods that tend to closely mirror what would happen on the job. The goal is often to establish (or perhaps change) employee behaviors, which entails demonstrating to individuals appropriate versus inappropriate behaviors. Role-playing is particularly useful because it allows the employees to practice appropriate behaviors and obtain feedback (i.e., debriefing) from instructors on what to do differently. Robert Sutton offers an example of how role-playing exercises allowed individuals at one organization to "get in the (others') shoes" in regards to incidents of workplace aggression. Hands-on methods such as this and others (e.g., behavior modeling, case studies) better enable the transfer of what was learned in training back to the job.

Many organizations approach harassment training (including sexual, racial, and religious harassment) using role playing and behavior modeling approaches, though the effectiveness of such training is unclear. At one bank, employees participated in annual training on the themes of "what is harassment?" and "how to address such situations" by watching examples on videotape and then having the opportunity to act out various scenarios with coworkers and instructors. A hotel chain engaged a consulting firm to develop scenarios to "act out," demonstrating to its employees what is and is not acceptable behavior. A discussion followed in the course of which training participants were asked questions related to the situation they had viewed, the perceptions and outcomes for the parties involved, and the procedure to follow should issues arise.

Of course, with the growing use of technology-based training, many organizations have turned to online delivery. At one organization, employees and supervisors receive online training related to workplace conduct on such topics as interpersonal dimensions of management, interpersonal communication skills, prevention of workplace violence, workplace diversity and effectiveness, and fair treatment. Because the training is online, modules can be completed at the individual's own pace and as the work schedule/workload permits (i.e., when the employee has some "down time"). The content is delivered via descriptions and definitions as well as interactive examples and case studies. The technology allows the organization to monitor whether and when the training has been completed. Trainee learning is evaluated through quizzes at the completion of each module. Employees who demonstrate insufficient understanding of critical concepts are redirected to additional training.

Training to Address Mistreatment

Training can also be useful in developing employee competencies to address nascent and existent issues of mistreatment. Individuals need some skills and knowledge of what to do should an issue arise prior to an incident occurring. This goes beyond simply educating employees about the availability of a dispute resolution system. While employee awareness of dispute resolution *options* and understanding of the benefits is necessary (though not sufficient) for the system to be utilized and effective, training is also needed to develop specific skills and competencies around dispute resolution. This would involve training focused on effectively navigating and communicating through the channels in a multi-step appeal process as well as mediation skills and effective negotiation and problem-solving techniques.

The need for particular skills and knowledge, and thus the focus of the training, will depend on the nature of an individual's job. For example, non-supervisory employees need to be trained in different dispute resolution techniques than employees in supervisory/management roles, and neither of these groups requires the dispute resolution skill set required of individuals in your organization who are formally tasked with resolving claims of mistreatment at work (e.g., ombudsmen, investigators, peer mediators, human resource professionals). These specialists require advanced skills training to manage the process of effective conflict resolution.

As previously noted, conflict can be positive for an organization, fostering opportunities for new ideas and creative solutions as well

---

Tips:
Possible Dispute Resolution Training Needs by Target Audiences

Employees	Team Leaders/ Supervisors	Dispute Resolution Experts/Third-Party Neutrals
• Awareness of conflict style • Communication (including active listening) • Problem-solving • Use of multi-step appeal process	• Awareness of conflict style • Communication • Problem-solving • Coaching • Decision-making • Mediation	• Coaching • Investigation • Mediation • Negotiation • Arbitration/ decision-making

as surfacing workplace policies and practices in need of clarification and/or modification. Training individuals in dispute resolution is therefore not about teaching people to avoid or minimize all conflict. Rather, the focus should be on providing people with the competencies to approach issues (or potential issues) constructively. This is similar to Robert Sutton's discussion of "teaching people how to fight."[15] While showing disrespect for others and engaging in personal attacks is never acceptable behavior, employees should have the knowledge and skills to confront and seek remedy for an issue of mistreatment.

Examining Reward Structures

As was noted by Steven Kerr in his seminal article in 1975 "On the folly of rewarding A, while hoping for B,"[16] all too often, the reward structures we have in place in our organizations may not be rewarding the behaviors we want to reward. Instead *the reward systems might be rewarding behaviors we actually do not want to occur in the workplace.* To that end, it is important to consider how your organization's reward policies and practices might serve to increase the occurrence of mistreatment or serve to prevent its successful resolution.

Questions to Ask

There are several questions you can ask about your current reward system including:

- *Does your evaluation and merit pay system reward for individual productivity only?* That is, are employees expected to cooperate and support one another, yet only get rewarded for how much they produce on their own? If so, this system could very well be rewarding employees who only "look out for number one" at the expense of the work group's or organization's overall functioning. Such behavior is likely to result in more incidents of mistreatment.

Case Scenario:
When Rewards Focus on Individual Production Only

Setting: A large, healthcare institution set up the performance evaluation of its IT staff to include the total number of work orders each staff member completed. This was originally done to encourage IT staff to complete work orders as quickly as possible. In addition, the healthcare institution implemented an incentive system such that IT staff with the highest number of work orders processed each quarter were rewarded with two paid days off.

Problem: Several months after the new program was implemented, the healthcare institution had an all-time high number of IT work orders requested. A number of departments complained that the IT systems were functioning very poorly and that this had created a number of problems with clients being billed incorrectly and admissions mishaps. In addition, several of the IT staff members had initiated complaints against one another claiming some staff members were hoarding hardware or were sabotaging one another in completing work orders (e.g., not passing along messages).

Source: Upon investigation it was revealed that a high number of these work orders were follow-ups to work orders that had been "fixed" initially, but not properly. It appeared that when IT staff members encountered a problem that they couldn't figure out on their own they no longer sought the advice of fellow staff members. Instead they would use a quick patch, presumably so they could take credit for the work. In addition, some staff members were so motivated to be the top performers they were actually hiding hardware from one another and withholding information.

Solution: The healthcare institution implemented several changes to address the problem. First, it included cooperation and team support in the performance evaluation. Although this had been identified as important during the job analysis, it was not linked properly to the evaluation. Second, it implemented a voice mechanism for feedback from others about the quality of the service provided in completing the work order. Finally, it modified the incentive system so that it took the feedback about the quality of the service into account and also provided scope for "shared credit" in completing a work order.

- *Do you have an incentive system or merit pay system that constrains the opportunities for reward or recognition?* That is, does your organization have a finite set of rewards, like a certain number of allowable "outstanding" evaluations or a fixed number of monetary awards? Such a system is likely to create competitiveness and ultimately dysfunctional behavior among employees as they vie for the rewards.

Case Scenario:
When Rewards Are Constrained

Setting: A consulting company had a policy to limit the number of "exceptional" performance ratings any one supervisor could allocate. The process was originally put in place to discourage supervisors from being lenient in their performance reviews (often to obtain large merit increases for their employees) and to motivate high performance among workers by "raising the bar" for what was deemed truly top performance.

Problem: A series of claims were made through the organization's grievance system regarding co-workers withholding pertinent information, "stealing" clients, and the like, in a sense "sabotaging" another employee's work performance. It seemed that competition rather than cooperation become commonplace in the organization.

Source: Upon investigation, the HR department heard many comments that such behavior was quite rational given the reward structure imposed upon managers. The biggest problems seemed to be in the workgroups that were historically the highest performing. Employees in such groups felt that if they were going to get ahead, and ultimately be rewarded, it was likely to be at the expense of a co-worker. They also heard many comments that the performance review system forced managers to provide invalid assessments of their employees. For example, managers felt they were forced to arbitrarily rate "exceptional" performers lower than they really were simply because one or more other employees had marginally higher performance. Other managers felt forced to rate average employees higher than they deserved simply because the overall workgroup was fairly mediocre. High-performing employees in high-performing workgroups were

Continued

particularly dissatisfied because they felt they were not evaluated accurately; the ratings were contingent not on their own performance, but on the "availability" of ratings allowed by the organization. In a sense, employees felt like they were "punished" for being part of a high-performing workgroup.

Solution: The organization repealed the rule, lifting the limitation on the number of exceptional ratings each manager could allocate. To help prevent managers from inflating their ratings of subordinate performance in the future, the organization requires managers to provide justification in writing (and with supporting evidence, where feasible) for any "above expectations" and "exceptional" ratings provided.

- *Does your evaluation and merit pay system focus on technical performance only?* If employees are not rewarded for how they interact with others in the workplace, they are unlikely to focus their attention on such behavior. Work behaviors related to teamwork, respect for others, and personal integrity could be reflected in the performance review to appraise and reward employees accordingly.

Case Scenario:
Performance Criteria Beyond Technical Proficiency

A small financial institution incorporated its organizational "value proposition" directly into its reward structure. All employees, including managers, were evaluated on how well they upheld the company's values (e.g., mutual respect, inclusiveness, integrity, openness) in addition to proficiency at their job. Half of the overall/final performance rating, which was the basis for merit raises and other administrative decisions (e.g., promotions, terminations), stemmed from an employee's performance on the "value" dimensions. Employees who were not rated as acceptable (or higher) on each of the company's value propositions would not be considered for supervisory positions without improvement. Managers who fell below acceptable standards were counseled and placed on probation until they demonstrated improvement.

Redesigning and Modifying Your Reward Structure

To the extent that your reward and recognition systems reflect the above elements, you may inadvertently facilitate mistreatment in the workplace. A careful assessment of your reward systems may reveal how the way you measure and reward behavior could be redesigned to prevent or at least minimize mistreatment. For example, performance appraisal methods that force raters to compare one individual's performance to that of others, such as a forced distribution or ranking method, may bring about behavior aimed at employee self-promotion over the betterment of the group. Such behavior can be particularly dysfunctional where job tasks within a workgroup are interdependent and/or your aim is to foster a team-based culture. Implementing a rating system which assesses and rewards collaborative and supportive workplace behaviors (e.g., the frequency with which the employee facilitated the contributions of other team members, the extent to which the employee demonstrated efforts to defuse conflict by using collaborative approaches) without forcing employees to compete for a fixed number of high ratings and/or rewards may be a more effective approach.

As another example, if you find that those employees deemed "high performers" in your organization (as reflected by performance ratings, merit raises, and/or promotions) are also demonstrating dysfunctional workplace behaviors, it may be that your performance management system is measuring and rewarding only the technical aspects of job performance (e.g., quantity of output or sales, initiative) without regard to interpersonal treatment of others. This would represent a deficiency in your system in that important aspects of workplace behavior are not being encouraged and are perhaps even being discouraged.

The bottom line is that individuals tend to engage in those behaviors that receive rewards and recognition. This suggests a particularly powerful opportunity to encourage the "right" workplace behaviors and minimize the chances for mistreatment by ensuring your performance measurement and reward system in fact defines, measures, and rewards such behavior. Yet it is quite easy to motivate the "wrong" behavior though a misalignment of the rewarded and the desired behavior.

Managerial Effectiveness in Preventing Mistreatment

Having the right people with the right tools in your management team is critical to preventing or minimizing the effects of mistreatment in your workplace. Effective managers can serve to prevent or minimize mistreatment by:

- ☑ Creating policies and procedures that are likely to be perceived as fair
- ☑ Soliciting voice and feedback from others before making critical decisions
- ☑ Applying policies and procedures consistently and without bias
- ☑ Using interpersonal and conflict resolution skills to resolve differences
- ☑ Serving as role models for how colleagues should treat one another
- ☑ Being knowledgeable about the resources available within and outside the organization
- ☑ Anticipating "hot issues" and heading off potential problems before they occur
- ☑ Responding to issues, as they arise, in a timely and appropriate way
- ☑ Fostering a civil work environment

Invest in the Careful Selection and/or Promotion of the "Right" Managers

Given the significant role of managers in defining, motivating, and developing employee behavior and the fact that a manager is often the first person to whom an employee would turn if he or she experienced mistreatment at work, it is clearly critical that individuals in such roles have the ability and willingness to foster an environment for their employees that discourages issues of mistreatment from developing. This reinforces the importance of selecting individuals for supervisory/managerial roles who are not simply competent in their task performance, but also effective in their interactions with others.

So how do you select the "right managers"? As described in the earlier section on recruitment and selection, there are several tools that are particularly good for screening out managers who are likely to instigate mistreatment. Again, you would need to follow the professional steps identified earlier for developing and validating a selection procedure (e.g., job analysis). The selection tools described earlier would also be useful for identifying whether someone has exhibited such skills in the past.

- Behavioral interviews
- Reference checks
- Assessment centers
- Performance evaluations (when making promotion decisions internally)

More specifically, performance criteria related to interacting with others and other interpersonal behaviors should be incorporated in your assessment centers, 360-degree performance appraisals, and the other evaluation tools in staffing for managerial positions.

Invest in Ongoing Training and Development of Managers

Certainly, as we emphasized earlier, training is important for all employees in preventing and/or reducing mistreatment in your organization. However, there are some additional training areas that would be particularly valuable for your management staff.

One content area that is often overlooked is *Fairness in Management.* The literature on justice provides a considerable amount of information about how individuals may arrive at a conclusion that they have been unfairly treated with respect to what outcomes they receive (distributive justice), the process used the make the decision (procedural justice), or the way they were treated interpersonally (interactional justice). Managers' behavior, as it relates to enhancing organizational justice, can have an important effect on employees' perceptions of mistreatment as well as their reactions to mistreatment if it occurs. Research has shown that perceptions of distributive justice and procedural justice serve to minimize the likelihood or magnitude of employees' negative reactions. The extent to which managers enhance interactional justice has been shown to be the strongest determinant of whether employees will respond aggressively toward a manager. Training in this area should contain certain elements:

Tips:
Fairness in Management

- Distributive Fairness
  - How people arrive at conclusions of distributive unfairness
  - The importance of "transparent communication" and "meeting expectations"[17]
  - How decisions can be made that minimize perceptions of distributive unfairness
  - How managers can better understand the outcomes valued by the people they supervise as well as what inputs they consider to be relevant
- Procedural Fairness
  - How people arrive at conclusions of procedural unfairness
  - How policies and procedures can be designed to minimize perceptions of procedural unfairness
  - How managers can develop, support and use voice mechanisms
- Interactional Fairness
  - How people arrive at conclusions of interactional unfairness
  - How managers can improve interactional fairness
  - How managers can effectively convey information and offer explanations for how decisions are made and the distribution of outcomes

Another content area that is particularly important for managerial development is leadership training. Both Leader-Member Exchange (LMX)[18] and Transformational Leadership[19] theories emphasize the quality of relationship between managers and employees. Leadership training focused on quality relationships between managers and the employees they supervise, as well as training in effective leadership traits and behaviors can be especially helpful for enhancing employees' perceptions of interactional justice.

Emphasize the Broader Organizational Good

To best develop a culture in which mistreatment is prevented or fully addressed when it does occur, it is critical that managers focus not only on their own department but also on what is in the best interests of the organization as a whole. For example, sometimes situations arise where a manager could and should address an issue within his or her department, yet the easiest way to address the situation is detrimental to other organizational units. In such a case, the issue has been addressed in the short-term, at least for a particular manager, but the root of the problem remains or even intensifies. In our experience, situations like the following are all too common within organizations.

Case Scenario:
Passing Issues on to Others

A manager at a state agency was challenged by a technically competent employee who caused continuous problems within the workgroup. This particular employee, "Sally," was known to "bully" others in the workgroup, creating a negative work culture and ultimately adversely affecting productivity and employee retention within the department. The manager was conflicted as to how to address the situation in part because Sally had a reputation within the organization as being a "high performer" and on the "fast-track" for a leadership position. Although the manager discussed the troublesome behaviors during the performance review meeting with Sally, the performance evaluation continued to reflect high job performance. When the manager was contacted by another department manager for a recommendation for someone to fill an opening as a supervisor, the manager saw this as his chance to rid his department of the "problem." The manager highlighted Sally's positive characteristics and did not mention the bullying issue. Sally was promoted to the new position, and new problems emerged. In a supervisory position, Sally had a much greater impact on those she supervised. Soon the turnover in Sally's department was at an all time high. However, Sally's new manager had a difficult time identifying the source of the problem as Sally continued to shine in other respects. It wasn't until several employees made oblique references to Sally's abrasive style during exit interviews that the new manager understood the source of the problem. By then a number of key employees had already left the company or transferred to other departments.

How can you ensure that managers act in the best interest of the overall organization? Clearly, incorporating interpersonal treatment and dispute resolution competency in staffing for and training of managers is critical. Yet there are specific considerations that may reflect whether managers will indeed emphasize the larger organization in responding to issues of mistreatment within their own department.

☑ Are managers held accountable for "passing on" and failing to address problems?

☑ Are managers evaluated and rewarded based on the culture within their department?

☑ Do managers have the command of their subordinates; that is, are they tough enough to take on problem subordinates?

☑ Do managers buy into and support organizational policies?

☑ Do managers have a handle on, communicate with, and have rapport with their employees?

We know of one company that has implemented several policies and practices which help to ensure managers will consider the larger organization. For example, one such policy is known as the "lemon law" in which managers who highly recommend an employee for a promotion may find that the employee is returned to their own department if his or her performance in the new department does not live up to the recommendation.

The Role of Disciplinary Actions and Terminations

The purpose of employee discipline is to stop undesired behavior and to encourage appropriate behavior. To the extent that mistreatment issues are the result of an employee's inappropriate behavior, employee discipline in addressing that behavior is relevant. Employee discipline, including terminations, helps to prevent mistreatment in two general ways. First, through correction and punishment, discipline modifies behavior. Second, by disciplining employees, you will send a signal to other employees that such behavior will not be tolerated.

Modifying Behavior through the Disciplinary Process

Virtually all organizations practice some form of progressive discipline. In contrast to traditional discipline, a progressive discipline program aims to gain employee cooperation with your organization's rules and expectations by basing the severity of the punishment on the nature of the offense and the number of times the offense has occurred. A typical progressive discipline process involves:

1. Verbal warning – a caution conveyed to the employee orally
2. Written warning – a warning provided in writing, with a copy sent to the human resource department to be included in the employee's personnel file
3. Suspension – a temporary layoff, sometimes with pay, while there is an ongoing investigation
4. Termination – an act by the organization to end the employment relationship

For serious offenses such as violence or threats of violence against others, the early and less stringent steps in the progressive discipline process can and should be skipped. The discipline system can be made most effective in those organizations following certain guidelines:

- Thoroughly investigate the situation
- Act early before the issue escalates or it appears you are condoning the behavior
- Apply disciplinary action consistently and fairly across employees
- Clearly explain what was inappropriate behavior and define appropriate behavior
- Provide the employee with resources (e.g., training) to address problem behavior
- Carefully document the process and results
- Follow-up to clarify expectations and ensure behavior has changed

Sending a Signal to Others through the Disciplinary Process

All the talk about interpersonal treatment in your workplace won't make much difference if your organization doesn't "walk the talk" in terms of taking action against chronic culprits of mistreatment in your workplace. When employees who engaged in mistreatment are disciplined, you also send a signal to other employees that mistreatment is not and will not be tolerated in the workplace. Conversely, by failing to discipline, you are in a sense condoning the inappropriate behavior. The fear of wrongful termination suits must be balanced against the costs of mistreatment in the workplace.

Overcoming Inertia

Despite the fact that many organizations have some form of progressive discipline in place, it is important to recognize that this doesn't necessarily mean that all managers and organizations are actually *using* the discipline process to address mistreatment problems. There may be a number of contributing factors for this lack of use, but our experience suggests some typical reasons:

- Managers who are conflict-avoidant and are uncomfortable discussing or responding to behavior problems.
- Organizations that do not support or reward managers who attempt to use progressive discipline.
- Managers' and organizations' concerns about how the employee might respond to the discipline including possibly violent reactions and litigation.

The previous discussions of preventing mistreatment (e.g., recruitment, selection, training, rewards) show how to address the first two bullet points. However, more needs to be said regarding the last one.

Addressing concerns about violent reactions

You may be concerned that disciplining an individual will lead to aggression or even violence. This concern is not unreasonable given that the individual may have engaged in deviant behavior to warrant the reprimand in the first place. As an extreme form of aggression, the threat of violence is particularly disconcerting given the potential for physical injury to those involved. Yet, as previously noted, failing to discipline simply out of fear of how the individual may react sends the wrong message to that individual and others in the organization – that such behavior will be tolerated!

Although the incidence of insider-initiated workplace violence (when someone inside the organization harms another organizational member) is the least prevalent of the types of workplace violence, it is receiving more attention because mistreatment in the form of organizational injustice "may be a key contributing factor to the act."[20] Research has offered several recommendations for preventing violent reactions in general, not just in response to discipline. Several of the recommendations for minimizing the threat of workplace violence have been discussed earlier, particularly enhancing organizational justice (including distributive, procedural, and interactional justice). Research has demonstrated the importance, in particular, of interactional justice in reducing retaliatory reactions, such as violence, to negative outcomes. The risk of workplace violence is also reduced in an organization that fully addresses issues of mistreatment.

If you are concerned that an individual will react with violence (or any form of aggression/abuse), it is even more critical to address the issue. Unfortunately employees' threats of workplace violence often get ignored. First and foremost, threats should be taken seriously. Please note that there are several workplace violence resources you should consult that go beyond our summary here, but below is a short summary of some tips for reducing risk of violence in administering discipline.

- Pay careful attention to how the information is conveyed. In particular, treating the employee with respect and dignity is critical.
- Attempt to prevent a potential situation by focusing on the individual's behavior, rather than making it seem personal (i.e., a "personal attack").
- Follow justice principles, including allowing the individual to voice his or her perspective.
- Speak to the individual with another person (e.g., HR manager) in the room.
- Alert organizational security to be on the lookout for a potential problem.

- If an individual threatens violence, take the threat seriously, alert security immediately (and local authorities when appropriate) and implement relevant crisis management plans.

Addressing litigation concerns
We are constantly learning of wrongful termination cases in which the plaintiffs were awarded hundreds of thousands or even millions of dollars. The fear of a case being filed, let alone of an award being made against your organization, is enough to give us pause before using discipline to address mistreatment problems.

There are, of course, ways to minimize or mitigate your litigation risk.

- ☑ Investigate claims, keeping in mind that there are often two sides (or more) to an issue.
- ☑ Document, document, document! It is critical that you keep a careful record of the investigation, performance issues, reports of mistreatment, disciplinary action, etc.
- ☑ Apply policies consistently across employees.
- ☑ Seek legal counsel. The time to seek legal counsel is *before* you make employment decisions such as terminations or demotions.

It is fairly easy to identify the potential consequences of taking disciplinary action against an employee. However, it is also important to give due consideration to what would happen if you did *not* take needed action. Questions to consider include:

- What litigation, related to this particular situation, are we vulnerable to if we do not take action (e.g., harassment claims)?
- What other economic consequences, related to this particular situation, could we experience if we do not take action (e.g., increased staff turnover, absenteeism, stress-related health problems, reduced productivity)?
- What other economic consequences in general could we experience if we do not take action (e.g., effect on culture, morale, productivity)

Good to Know:
Key Points

- Nothing is fail-proof when it comes to preventing mistreatment, but through careful and purposeful design of workplace practices, you can better ensure that you have a culture that is less tolerant of, and certainly does not promote, mistreatment.

- Through effective employee selection, you may be able to head off potential mistreatment prior to employees even joining the organization.

- Training to prevent, minimize, and address mistreatment should focus on orienting and socializing newcomers, training employees on appropriate vs. inappropriate workplace conduct, and training on how to address mistreatment.

- It is important to consider how your organization's reward policies and practices might serve to increase the occurrence of mistreatment in the workplace or might serve to prevent its successful resolution by rewarding the "wrong" behaviors.

- Given the significant role of managers in defining, motivating, and developing employee behavior, it is critical that individuals in such roles have the ability and willingness to prevent mistreatment from developing or minimize its occurrence.

- Employee discipline helps to prevent mistreatment by modifying behavior and encouraging appropriate behavior and by sending a signal to other employees that such behavior will not be tolerated.

Chapter 5

Getting Started on Designing Effective Dispute Resolution Systems

Granted, a certain amount of conflict at work is inevitable and some types of conflict are desirable. However, perceptions of mistreatment in the workplace are expensive, and having an appropriate system to address mistreatment when it does occur is beneficial to both your organization and your employees. Not only do such systems serve to address or resolve mistreatment, they are also an important part of preventing mistreatment in the first place.

But how can you develop a system that addresses mistreatment in the workplace once it has occurred while also potentially preventing other mistreatment from occurring? Fortunately, there is a considerable amount of information from best practices and carefully conducted research that speaks to this very issue. In this chapter, you will learn how to start the process of creating the best evidence-based practices in both stand-alone (i.e., single) and comprehensive (i.e., multiple and integrated) mistreatment resolution procedures. Consistent with research and practice in this area, we will refer to such a system as a "dispute resolution system."

As noted earlier, if you have a unionized workforce, you would typically negotiate how collective bargaining violations will be addressed through a particular dispute resolution system and any changes to the system would need to be made through collective bargaining. However, the information in the next few chapters can provide guidance for identifying what you would like to have included in such an agreement. Also, you may be able to have a dispute resolution system for addressing concerns that do not fall under the collective bargaining agreement.

Why Bother?

Designing and maintaining an effective mistreatment management system takes work. It may be tempting to ask, why bother spending all this effort on addressing mistreatment? Shouldn't you just focus on preventing it instead? But, even with the very best efforts to prevent mistreatment, your organization will still have some employees who feel mistreated in some way. Consider if you did not have any means to resolve an employee's perception of mistreatment, what would likely happen? We know that when someone feels mistreated they may react to this perception in a number of ways including:

Psychologically: emotional reactions such as anger, fear, rejection[1] (often intense); over time the result is likely to be a change in work attitudes such as reduced job satisfaction or lower organizational commitment.[2]

Behaviorally: reduced productivity, increased absences, turnover, or acts of sabotage or theft.

Physiologically: stressor type reactions including physiological symptoms (e.g., high blood pressure, sleeping difficulty).

These reactions often worsen over time when the original mistreatment is not addressed or resolved. Research and practice has demonstrated that having an effective system to address mistreatment can help reduce these adverse reactions considerably, and ultimately serve to reduce the toll taken by mistreatment on your bottom line.

Initial Steps

There are several initial steps you should take before implementing a dispute resolution system.

Good to Know: Initial Steps	
• Identify goals for dispute resolution system • Create a design team	• Identify venues for voice • Examine key considerations

Identify Goals

First it is important to identify the goals your organization wants to achieve through designing and implementing a dispute resolution system. Doing so will provide guidance for making early decisions (e.g., examining key considerations) and will later allow you to identify how you should measure the effectiveness of your system once it has been implemented. Also, if your organization has multiple goals (or criteria) it would be helpful to identify their relative priorities before beginning the process of evaluating the available alternatives.

Organizations implement dispute resolution systems for a variety of reasons and, accordingly, evaluate their effectiveness in a variety of ways. Some organizations implement such systems to improve organizational attractiveness for recruitment purposes or to stem potential union organizing attempts. Others are more interested in addressing mistreatment or reducing the costs incurred when employees experience mistreatment in the workplace. For illustrative purposes, four goals that might be set for dispute resolution systems consistent with the purpose of this book are identified next. Note that some organizations have only one of the goals identified below; others have multiple goals.

A system that successfully addresses employee mistreatment. This goal would be achieved when employees who actually use your system to address a perceived mistreatment feel that their complaint has been effectively resolved. In addition, the other parties involved (e.g., another disputant, a dispute resolution professional) should feel satisfied by the resolution as well.

A system that is perceived as fair. The goal here is that members of the organization should perceive the system to be fair in terms of how it is set up and how it operates, regardless of whether or not they have used the system. This would mean, presumably, that they would be willing to use the system should they experience mistreatment in the workplace. It would also mean that employees are more accepting of the outcome, regardless of whether the outcome is favorable for a particular individual. With this goal you would assess the reactions of both users and nonusers toward the system.

A system that is cost-effective. The costs of mistreatment in the workplace are well documented. To work toward this goal, the costs of the new system (e.g., administrative costs, average time to resolve, external resources required, resulting litigation) are compared against either the costs of a previous system or those of not having a system implemented.

A system that handles a broad range of issues and constituents. Previous research has found that some systems are generally more suited to certain types of mistreatment or may be more favored by certain employees. However, you would, of course, want your system to be used by members throughout your organization, and you would want it to be able to handle the varying types of mistreatment experienced by your employees. Examining the way in which the system is used, in terms of demographics of employees and the type of mistreatment addressed, would determine how successful you had been in achieving this goal.

Creating a Design Team

After identifying your goal(s) for implementing a dispute resolution system, you should then create a Design Team who will serve as the steering committee for this change. There are a number of factors that you should consider in forming such a team.

- Who in the organization has the necessary skill or knowledge in the following areas?
  - Expertise in conflict management
  - Familiarity with the types of mistreatment experienced by organizational members
  - Knowledgeability about legal constraints (e.g., industry-related, union-related) that affect how your organization can create a dispute resolution system

- Who would help with "buy-in" to the new system?
  - Particular levels of employee representation (e.g., non-management, supervisors)
  - Key departments that would (likely) help administer the system (e.g., human resources, legal)
- Who would facilitate the dynamics of the design team?
  - Are there any "bridgers," who would bring various facets of the organization together?
  - Who has good communication, interpersonal, and mediation skills?

Typically, we find that the sizes of these design teams vary from 5 to 12 members. As is the case with any task force or work team, the size and makeup of the team would vary depending on your organization's unique needs (e.g., you may have multiple areas for which it is critical to have representation) or constraints (e.g., required union representation as laid out in collective bargaining agreement). However, it is important to keep in mind that larger teams would make it more difficult to meet face to face, due to conflicting schedules, and may make it more difficult to keep everyone up to speed. Virtual meetings, conference calls, and other technology-based meeting tools can be used in place of face-to-face meetings, particularly for larger design teams or for those which have members who do not physically work near one another, as in multinational corporations.

Identify Venues for Voice

The purpose of the Design Team is to create a system to provide voice for mistreated employees. To that end, it is critical to identify how your team will solicit voice during the process of developing the system. We know that employees should be provided with the opportunity to "voice" their ideas on how to voice mistreatment because we know from both research and experience that it is likely to lead to higher acceptance of the dispute resolution system, higher perceptions of its fairness, and to a system of a type that is appropriate to your organization. There are a number of informal and formal means to do this. Ideally you would use more than one method to solicit voice.

- You might simply announce the project and encourage members of the organization to share concerns and ideas with the team members.
- You could use a simple suggestion box to solicit ideas.
- You could allow time during the meetings for members to share their ideas.
- You could conduct an employee survey, soliciting ideas related to the system.

Case Scenario:
One Company's Approach to Soliciting Voice for Designing a System

The two HR professionals in a rapidly growing, family-owned business convinced the owners that they needed to develop a dispute resolution system. The HR professionals had heard from a number of employees who had mistreatment concerns but these employees were not comfortable talking to their managers about it because there were family relationships among some key people.

Understanding the importance of soliciting voice in the design of such a system, the business elected to use a novel, technology-based way to develop the system. Specifically, an electronic bulletin board (housed in an off-site server) was created for the purpose of developing the system. In phase I, the board had several open-ended questions posted to initiate the discussion such as: What do you think is needed in the system so you would be willing to use it if you needed to? How should the final decisions be made? Employees (who were technology-savvy) could post their responses anonymously.

In Phase II, the consultant posted a draft of a proposed system that incorporated the concerns identified in Phase I. The system was revised and modified further until there appeared to be a consensus among the employees. Not only did this approach result in a system that was accepted by employees, it also served to identify several other issues (e.g., common mistreatment issues) that should be addressed in the personnel policies.

Examine Key Considerations

As is to be discussed later, the contemporary best practice is to develop a comprehensive system that can address all or a wide range of mistreatment types. However, that may not be immediately practical for your organization, in which case you would want to first focus on designing a system that is most appropriate for your organization's needs today. There are several factors that you should carefully consider before designing or modifying your system.

Tips:
Questions to Ask Before You Begin

☑ What types of mistreatment do I generally need to address?

☑ What are my employees' preferences with respect to types of resolution procedures?

☑ How important is confidentiality (or anonymity) to my employees?

☑ What legal and contractual concerns do I need to address with the resolution procedure?

Types of mistreatment?

One important question to consider is what *types* of mistreatment are most likely to be experienced by employees in your organization so that you can design your system accordingly. Information you gleaned from your scanning sources can be particularly helpful in answering this question. In addition, you might consider how not being able to implement certain workplace practices helpful in preventing mistreatment (as discussed in Chapter 4) could make certain types of mistreatment more likely. Research has demonstrated that the type of perceived mistreatment is a relevant factor in how employees prefer to resolve or address the mistreatment. For example, employees prefer to use more formal, adjudicative procedures (e.g., grievance procedure, arbitration) for mistreatment that is more legalistic in nature, such as discrimination or a contract violation. If your organization is going through changes that are particularly likely to result in the perception of this type of mistreatment (e.g., contract changes, layoffs, reduced promotion opportunities), then it would be especially important to include these type of dispute resolution procedures in your plan.

Another reason you should consider the types of mistreatment likely to be experienced in your organization is that the way in which employees characterize the mistreatment also affects how they *react* to the mistreatment. For example, we know that employees respond differently to mistreatment that they think was caused by someone's discretionary actions ("personalized" or "individualized") versus a general policy that was uniformly applied to everyone. In particular, employees have stronger, more negative responses (e.g., more job withdrawal) to individualized mistreatment. If your organization has had, or is likely to have, this type of mistreatment, then it would be important to include a means to carefully address the post-dispute relationship (e.g., restorative justice) between the employee and whoever he or she thinks caused the mistreatment.

Employee preferences?
If an employee has the option of choosing a way to address mistreatment, there are a number of factors that will likely affect that employee's choice or preference. Some of these factors have to do with the existence and reputation of the dispute resolution procedure and will be discussed later. However, other factors vary according to the composition and nature of your specific workforce and include such things as:

- *The relationship between employees and managers/others.* Employees who have strong, trusting relationships with their managers or with whoever is the source of the mistreatment prefer to use procedures that are less formal or less adversarial. This is particularly true when the employees have had positive experiences working things out with the others in the past. If there is a heightened level of acrimony between management and employees (perhaps evidenced by a climate survey or other information from your scanning sources), formal procedures might be the most immediate need for your organization.
- *The amount of employee loyalty to the organization.* If your workforce is characterized by high loyalty or high attachment to the organization, it is especially important to include dispute resolu-

tion procedures that allow employees to work out perceptions of mistreatment informally or with a neutral third party. Thus, an organization characterized by strong relationships among employees and strong levels of loyalty to the organization may be able to focus on more informal or consensual/collaborative approaches.

Organizational structure

Another factor to consider is the structure of your organization. For example, are the culture and the reporting relationships in your organization hierarchical? If so, a hierarchical dispute resolution may work there. On the other hand, if your organization is fairly flat and is characterized by self-managed work groups, it may be appropriate to include dispute resolution procedures which allow parties more control over the final decision.

Importance of confidentiality

Offering dispute resolution options that maintain confidentiality may be desirable given that employees tend to be more comfortable using such systems. Offering an option which allows for anonymity is also something to consider carefully. This may be particularly feasible when mistreatment has affected a number of individuals. However, the importance of confidentiality and thus the extent to which confidentiality is integrated throughout your system may vary depending on your organization's situation. For example, in organizations characterized by particularly acrimonious work cultures, confidentiality may be critical and anonymity preferable to facilitate employee confidence in and use of the system. Of course, employees would need to have enough trust in the organization to believe in the assurance of confidentiality! Confidentiality may also be particularly important if retaliation against employees using the system is a concern.

Legal and contractual concerns

Finally, before designing a dispute resolution system, you should identify if there are any particular legal or contractual concerns that affect your organization in particular. For example, your industry may be subject to a particular statute that requires internal investigations of certain types of mistreatment. Similarly, your job offers may include a due process clause that requires certain dispute resolution procedures to be followed before an employee is disciplined or discharged. Or, your workforce may be unionized and the collective bargaining agreement may require that you offer a certain type of grievance procedure to address violations of the agreement.

In the next two chapters, the types of stand-alone systems and comprehensive systems will be described. In addition, we outline the process used to design such systems and give examples. With all these explanations it is assumed that you have already undertaken the initial steps described in this chapter.

Good to Know:
Key Points

- Having an effective dispute resolution system is an important step to preventing and reducing adverse reactions to mistreatment in the workplace.
- The process of designing a dispute resolution system begins with the identification of your organization's goals for such a system.

- Next, you should create a design team and identify venues for employee input into the process.
- The design of a dispute resolution system should take into account the types of mistreatment prevalent in your organization, employee preferences, the importance of confidentiality, and legal and contractual constraints.

Chapter 6

Dispute Resolution System Options

There are a variety of stand-alone dispute resolution system approaches that can be created and implemented in the workplace. These approaches *differ* from one another in several respects, but most notably they vary in terms of these two factors:

- Level of formality – the extent to which an approach is documented and requires following certain steps.
- Consensuality – the extent to which the parties to the mistreatment have control over how the mistreatment is resolved.

In this section, you will become familiar with the major types of dispute resolution systems, their benefits and drawbacks, and how you would design and implement such systems in your workplace. At the end of the chapter, some common concerns across dispute resolution systems will be discussed, including ensuring

Good to Know: Major Types of Dispute Resolution Systems	

• Informal Discussion
• Open Door
	• Third-Party Facilitation
	   ◦ Mediation
	      ▪ Internal
	      ▪ External
	   ◦ Ombudspersons
	• Multi-Step Appeal Systems

organizational justice, conducting workplace investigations, and minimizing retaliation.

Informal Discussion

Definition

With this method, the mistreated employee tries to address the mistreatment by talking directly with the person who is considered to be the cause of it. That is, the employee "talks things out" with the manager or coworker and they try to reach some mutually acceptable solution. This method is informal, as it can be done privately, with no documentation. It is also consensual because the parties have control over the possible solution as well as whether they will accept it. Given its informality, it may at first appear to not be an actual system, per se. However, for many organizations it is the only dispute resolution method in place. Further, because of its inherent informality, this approach may act as a first step to a more formal process, it may be recommended or even required that employees try this approach first, or it may be the only acceptable approach in the organization. Below are some examples.

Examples:
Informal Discussion

- An international pharmaceutical company has a conflict resolution policy that strongly urges its associates to try to "work things out" by talking with the other person(s) first before pursuing other alternatives.
- A union of professional employees has a grievance procedure that calls for a good faith attempt to resolve issues through informal discussion before filing a written grievance.
- A small printing company's policy is that all conflicts among employees should be addressed by the following: 1) whoever has a complaint should share that complaint, face-to-face, with the person that either caused the problem or has the ability to address the problem; 2) all organizational members should treat each other with the highest respect and courtesy whether they are making or receiving the complaint; 3) the discussion should continue between those parties until it is resolved.

Design, Implementation, and Maintenance

Often, the informal discussion approach exists merely because it is included as an organization's conflict resolution policy. Organizations, that is to say, often have a policy that problems, issues, or conflicts should be worked out between the disputing parties and do little, if anything, beyond including this policy in an employee handbook. Whether employees choose to use this approach will depend to a large extent on whether the following four conditions are met:

- Employees are aware of the policy.
- The organizational culture supports the policy.
- There is a minimum amount of trust between the mistreated employee and whoever the employee feels is the source of the mistreatment.
- Employees believe they have the skills to use this approach.

However, you can make this approach a viable method in your organization by following these steps outlined below.

☑ *Design a clear policy that indicates when employees should use informal discussion to address a mistreatment concern.* There may be some situations (e.g., workplace violence) where you do not want employees to attempt informal discussion first. Include this policy in the orientation materials, employee handbook, and related materials.

☑ *Communicate the policy to all employees.* Evidence-based practice has identified that including the policy in an employee handbook is simply not enough communication; it needs to be reinforced through other avenues as well. For example, it might be appropriate to remind employees of this option when discussing some organizational change (e.g., benefits).

☑ *Provide communication, conflict resolution, and negotiation training to all employees.* The success of this approach depends on the parties' abilities to communicate effectively and reach successful resolution while still treating one another with respect. Employees will be more likely to initiate such an approach if they feel they have the requisite skills.

☑   *Ensure your organization's culture supports informal discussion.*
Organizations that have a norm against discussing differences
or speaking up would most likely not be able to take advantage of the informal discussion approach. Also organizations
in which confidentiality is regularly breached would not be
good candidates either.

Benefits

Research has documented a number of benefits of the informal discussion method as a way of addressing mistreatment. Because it is
readily accessible, with no documentation required, it can serve to
address mistreatment quickly and save or prevent a considerable
amount of costs. In addition, our empirical research has shown that
those who use this approach successfully are generally much more
satisfied with the outcome than those who use other approaches successfully. This is particularly true for more loyal employees. Finally,
there is some evidence that this informal approach, when it leads to
successful resolution, is less likely to result in retaliation against the
mistreated employee.

Good to Know:
Benefits of Informal Discussion

- Little time delay
- If resolution is reached, least costly method
- Higher satisfaction, particu-larly for loyal employees
- Less likely to result in re-taliation

Drawbacks

There are certainly some potential drawbacks as well. Some types of
mistreatment may be too severe (e.g., bullying, harassment) or too
volatile in nature (e.g., violence or threats of violence) for this
approach. That is, the accusation may be of too serious a nature, or
it might simply be dangerous, for the situation to be discussed without

others present. Also, if one or both parties do not have adequate communication or conflict resolution skills, an informal discussion could exacerbate or escalate the mistreatment, making it even more difficult to resolve it successfully through other methods. A defensive reaction, from either party, could result in greater polarization. For example, if the nature of the complaint is that an individual's supervisor is verbally abusive, talking directly with the supervisor may not be an effective way to address the issue. Adequate communication skills and a supportive culture are paramount for the success of this approach; if not done properly, it could actually make things worse.

Tips	
Dos of Informal Discussion	*Don'ts of Informal Discussion*
• DO provide and communicate a clear policy • DO provide training on communication and conflict resolution	• DO NOT use informal discussion in an organization that does not have a culture to support its use • DO NOT use informal discussion in potentially volatile situations

Open-Door System

Definition

An open-door system is a dispute resolution method in which a mistreated employee can approach any level of management, present the situation, and ask to have it addressed. With this method, the employee can usually appeal that manager's decision to higher management levels until he or she has exhausted all levels (typically on reaching the CEO level). The term "open-door" is used to represent the idea that all doors are open and he or she has the option of approaching any level of management with the situation and can even skip levels if desired.

Example:
IBM's Open Door Policy

International Business Machines (IBM) is well-known for its open-door policy that was created in the 1920s and formalized as policy in the 1950s. IBM's open-door policy was considered to be a direct outgrowth of one of IBM's core beliefs: respect for the individual.

Below is IBM's open-door policy as it appeared in the early 1990s:[1]

> Should you have a problem which you believe the company can help solve, discuss it with your immediate manager, your manager's manager, your personnel manager, or your branch or site manager. You will find that a frank talk with your manager is usually the easiest way to deal with the problem.

> If the matter is not resolved or is of such a nature that you prefer not to discuss it with your location management, you should go to the senior management in your business unit.

> Finally, if you feel that you still have not received a satisfactory answer, you may cover the matter with the chairman by mail, or personally if the chairman finds it appropriate to the resolution.

Design, Implementation, and Maintenance

This approach is extremely common in organizations, to the point where some consider saying "we have an open-door policy" to be a cliché. What distinguishes the "talk" from "walking the talk" is how the open-door policy is designed, implemented, and maintained. The success of this approach depends, in particular, on the following factors:

- Managers have been well-trained, possess the skills to respond appropriately, and can maintain confidentially (as far as possible).
- The organizational culture supports the policy.
- The system is considered credible and has a good reputation in the organization.

Given its inherent flexibility and, to some extent, informality, several of the steps are quite similar to those needed to make an effective informal discussion method work. However, it is less consensual in that others, besides the disputing parties, have control over the decision. You can maximize the potential benefits of the open-door approach and minimize the drawbacks of this approach by following these steps.

☑ Design a clear policy that describes how the open door system works. Employees should be made aware of:
  • Who they can approach and whether they are required to go in a specific order.
  • Whether and to whom they can appeal.
  • What step is the "final" appeal.
  • What information will be kept confidential (and not) and between whom.
  • What steps are taken to protect them against retaliation (see section on Auditing Retaliation below).

☑ As is the case with informal discussion, there may be some situations (e.g., workplace violence) where you do not want employees to present complaints in this manner to particular individuals. It would be important to include this policy in the orientation materials, employee handbook, and related materials.

☑ Include a "no retaliation" component to the policy and implement mechanisms to ensure protection for both the mistreated employee and whoever is considered by the employee to be the cause of the mistreatment (see Auditing Retaliation below).

☑ Communicate the policy to employees, managers, and anyone else who might use the system or be involved in the process.

☑ Provide periodic communication and conflict resolution training to all managers. This system means that any manager could have an employee (who may or may not be a direct report) walk in the office and ask to have something resolved. How managers respond to this is critical to reaching an early and effective resolution. It is also important that managers are aware of what issues may need to be referred to a higher level or other party (e.g., human resources) due to the severity or sensitivity of the complaint (e.g., claims of sexual harassment, threats or acts of violence).

☑ Ensure your organization's culture is consistent with this type of system (see Chapter 4). If there are strong norms against speaking up, "making waves," or "going above" your manager, then it may be very difficult to make this approach successful in your organization.

Benefits

When an open-door system is operating at its best, it can provide several benefits. First, open-door systems can provide a means for members of an organization, including management, to engage in an open dialogue about issues in the workplace. Open-door systems can also provide a way to address mistreatment without incurring expenses from outside expertise. Finally, the skills and processes used in an open-door system for addressing workplace mistreatment could also be used to address issues with clients or other businesses.

Drawbacks

Despite its general popularity as a system, open-door systems are notorious for several potential drawbacks. As with the informal discussion method, the mistreatment can sometimes escalate when this approach is used. Most notably, there is considerable evidence that such systems are linked to heightened retaliation, particularly against the employee who claims mistreatment as well. Also, given it is informal in nature, there may be little or no documentation of the use of this approach, creating even more vulnerability to litigation.

Tips	
Dos of Open-Door System	*Don'ts of Open-Door System*
• DO provide and communicate a clear policy • DO provide periodic training on communication and conflict resolution • DO provide a clear means for protecting employees against retaliation	• DO NOT use open-door systems in an organization that avoids conflict or punishes employees for speaking "out of turn" • DO NOT use open-door systems in potentially volatile situations

Third-Party Facilitation

There are a number of approaches in which a third-party, someone not a direct party to the mistreatment, can serve to facilitate the successful resolution of a perceived mistreatment. Indeed, research has found that third-party facilitators who are perceived to have expertise "can be effective in mediating workplace conflicts, particularly when disputants must make significant concessions."[2] The two primary approaches include mediation and the use of an ombudsperson. Although there are a number of variations or hybrids of these approaches, they do share several common features.

- A neutral, third-party is used.
- Neutral third-parties have undergone some formal training.
- Parties to the mistreatment maintain control over the solution or resolution of the mistreatment.

Mediation

Like informal discussion, mediation is a collaborative, consensual approach that allows both the mistreated employee and the other party to maintain control over how the issue is resolved. However, this approach offers the addition of a mediator, someone who is trained to listen to both parties and identify potential solutions that the two parties might not otherwise identify. Often a mediator will do the following:

- Meet separately with each party and discuss their underlying concerns. The mediator's neutral role may allow him or her to uncover underlying issues that neither party would necessarily be willing to state directly to the other party.
- Maintain confidentiality with both parties and instead use the gained information to shape the course of the discussion or make recommendations.
- Serve as a buffer or go-between in particularly contentious situations in which the mistreated employee and other party's communication has broken down.

An important question to ask is how do you find appropriate mediators that can serve in this role in your organization? The answer to this question depends on whether you plan to use internal or external mediators for addressing such mistreatment complaints. The advantages and disadvantages of mediation also vary by type of mediator used.

Internal Mediation

Internal mediators are usually selected from current employees and developed as mediators by the organization. The most common internal mediator, particularly in the public sector, is known as a peer mediator. Peer mediators are employees who continue to perform their original job, but also serve as mediators in situations where there is no clear conflict of interest (e.g., outside their own department). Peer mediators usually undergo a one-week training program, either internally or externally. Often peer mediation programs are limited to addressing particular types of mistreatment that do not generally have statutory implications.

Example:
Colorado's Voluntary State Employee Mediation Program (SEMP)

Colorado has used a peer mediation program for its state employees since 1986. The online description of the program provides detailed information about how the program works as well as how peer mediators are trained. Below are some excerpts from their stated policy:[3]

- "Mediators for the program are current state employees who have received formal mediation training and who volunteer their time to the program with the approval of their supervisors. These trained and experienced mediators are employed in a number of different occupations and departments throughout state government and represent diverse backgrounds.
- Employees and supervisors are encouraged to request mediation in situations where interpersonal disputes are significantly disruptive, and where other means of resolution have proven ineffective.
- Mediation is voluntary except in situations where a grievance has been filed. In these cases, if one party asks for mediation '...the other party must participate and time limits are

---

suspended pending the outcome or discontinuance of mediation.' (8-9B)

- Mediators are neutral impartial facilitators who help the parties arrive at a mutually agreeable solution. They may not impose their views or solutions to a problem nor act as advocates for either party.
- Mediators are required to keep confidential all information obtained in a mediation process and all notes and other materials generated in the mediation process are destroyed.
- Mediators are required to report any statements regarding harm to anyone as well as statements suggesting that a serious crime will be committed. Reports will be made to the Mediation Administrator.
- Final agreements will vary from case to case but all final agreements will require that both parties sign the agreement for it to be in force. Agreements will indicate how the parties plan to implement the agreement, and how they will involve and communicate the plan to the supervisor.

Mediation Process

- Generally, mediators may not be assigned to mediate a dispute in the department where the mediator is employed.
- Normally, mediation is limited to four sessions. If the mediator believes additional sessions would produce an agreement, additional sessions may be held.

Quality Assurance

- Only those mediators who have completed appropriate training and have approval from their supervisor will be allowed to mediate. The 40-hour basic course given by the Colorado Division of Human Resources will qualify. The Mediation Administrator will consider other courses on a case-by-case basis.
- Refresher training will be made available periodically to those in the mediator pool. The training will be designed to assure quality performance by mediators. Refresher training will be required for those who wish to continue in the mediator pool.
- The parties to the mediation will complete an evaluation at the end of each mediation assignment. Continuation in the mediation pool is contingent on receiving adequate evaluations. In addition, the Administrator may observe mediations and complete a written evaluation of the mediator(s)."

Design, Implementation and Maintenance
As is illustrated in the Colorado example, a number of questions need to be addressed in developing such a method in your organization. Design a thorough policy that addresses, at a minimum the following questions:

- ☑ Who is eligible to serve as a peer mediator? Selection of appropriate mediators is a key success factor and should be treated with the same care as other staffing decisions.
- ☑ What types of mistreatment can be addressed by this method? You may want to avoid forms of mistreatment that require advanced knowledge of EEO legislation as well as those where how the matter is handled in mediation could have implications for subsequent litigation.
- ☑ How will an individual mediator be assigned to mediate a particular situation?
- ☑ What kind of records will be kept and how will confidentiality be maintained?
- ☑ How will you handle a situation when only one party wants mediation?

You should then proceed to:

- Design or find an appropriate training mechanism for mediators. The standard one-week training session has been criticized as being too short, so consider expanding beyond a one week. You will also need to develop a plan for how mediators can maintain or further develop their mediation skills.
- Communicate the new system to current organizational members.
- Provide a means for those who use the system to provide feedback about the mediator and the system. For example, this could be done with a post-mediation survey.

Benefits
There are several possible benefits to using or offering a peer/employee mediation method. As is the general case with mediation methods, it can save time and money by resolving a mistreatment without pursuing external means (e.g., litigation). Peer mediators' familiarity with

the organizational context may give them a "leg up" in understanding the nuances of the perceived mistreatment. Peer mediators may be able to provide useful feedback to the organization about the general types of mistreatment issues experienced by employees. Finally, there are several experienced organizations that assert this approach results in high satisfaction among employees who use it.

Drawbacks
This approach also has drawbacks. One concern raised by practitioners and researchers is whether peer mediators are truly trained enough to work as mediators. The standard one-week training course in particular has been criticized as too little to be effective. Another issue is the amount of administrative time required to oversee this process.

Tips	
Dos of Peer Mediation	*Don'ts of Peer Mediation*
• DO communicate the policy to all employees • DO provide thorough (more than one week) and follow-up training (periodic training afterward) to peer mediators • DO evaluate the method's effectiveness	• DO NOT assume all employees will be effective as peer mediators • DO NOT use peer mediators when specialized knowledge (e.g., of EEO legislation) is required

External Mediation
Another type of mediation is the use of trained, qualified mediators who are external to your organization. Typically, such mediators have extensive training and/or experience that they can use to effectively facilitate a successful resolution of the mistreatment. For example, you might use the services of mediators who are listed with the American Arbitration Association, which requires them to have a certain level of ongoing training, experience, and positive evaluations. Generally, the use of external mediation is voluntary and it is up to the parties whether or not they will attempt to resolve an issue

through mediation. However, sometimes external mediation can be court-ordered, for example, before proceeding to litigation.

Example:
EEOC and Major Corporations Partner for Mediation

In 1999, the EEOC implemented its National Mediation Program with the aim of resolving workplace disputes more amicably and quickly than through a formal EEOC investigation or litigation. Examples of companies signing a Universal Agreement to Mediate (UAM) include Intel, Halliburton, ConAgra Foods, Ford Motor Company, CenterPoint Energy, McDonalds USA, Albertsons, International Dairy Queen, Johns Hopkins Health Systems, Golden Corral Corp., and Southern Company. Under the terms of a UAM, all eligible charges of discrimination filed with the EEOC naming the partner company as the employer/respondent are referred to the EEOC's mediation unit. From 1999 through 2007, over 98,000 mediations were held with nearly 68,000 charges (69%) successfully resolved.[4]

Design, Implementation, & Maintenance
There are several key issues to address before implementing an external mediation system in your organization.

☑ What types of mistreatment can be addressed by external mediation? As with internal mediation, there may be some types of mistreatment that would not be appropriate for external mediation. However, depending on the expertise of the mediator, it may be appropriate to include some types of statutory mistreatment.

☑ How will confidentiality be ensured? External mediators may learn about incriminating information while discussing issues separately with the parties. Given the range of legal regulations in different geographic areas, it would be prudent to investigate what confidentiality concerns are relevant in your area as well as how to, possibly, draft an appropriate confidentiality agreement.

☑ How will the mediator be selected? That is, how will the pool of qualified mediators be identified (e.g., through a respected authority)? Also, how will a particular mediator be selected for a given case? One common practice is to allow the two parties to eliminate mediators one by one (alternating) from a randomly generated list, until only one remains.

Benefits
There are several benefits to this approach. Again, because the parties still retain control over the resolution of the mistreatment, it is more likely to result in a solution that is acceptable to both parties. Also, external mediation allows the use of an external expert, who might be viewed as more credible by the parties, yet it does so while protecting the confidentiality of the mistreated employee and the other party. There is also considerable evidence that it is significantly less costly in terms of both time and money relative to other external procedures, such as litigation.

Drawbacks
There are drawbacks to external mediation as well. One drawback is the success of this approach depends on both parties making a good faith effort to reach an agreement. This may be difficult depending on the relationship of the parties and the nature of the mistreatment. Also, an external mediator is not an insider, and therefore does not have the same organizational knowledge that an internal mediator would have.

Ombudspersons

Another type of third-party-facilitated method is the use of ombudspersons. Ombudsperson is the job title of someone who is a designated neutral manager in the organization and who reports directly to the CEO outside the regular chain of command. An ombudsperson usually has received advanced, specialized training and typically performs a wide variety of tasks, all with the ultimate goal of facilitating resolution of a mistreatment issue without imposing his or her own solution. To that end, an ombudsperson may pursue a number of approaches including such activities as:

- Listening to the mistreated employee's and the other party's versions of the situation

- Identifying possible methods to address the situation
- Gathering information to help in the resolution of the issue
- Mediating informally between the parties
- Coaching the parties in communication, negotiation, or other needed skills to reach resolution

All of these responsibilities are carried out with the utmost attention to maintaining confidentiality. In addition to addressing employment disputes, many ombudspersons are also responsible for facilitating the resolution of complaints of other constituents such as clients, customers, or the public.

Example:
Ombudsperson at Stanford University

Stanford University's Ombuds Program provides an excellent example of the use of an ombudsperson in an organization to address mistreatment concerns. The Ombuds Program has a website that provides comprehensive information about how the program works, including:[5]

- A brief overview of what the program provides, with links to more detailed information on the following as well
- An introduction to the ombudsperson, including his or her background and training
- A description of the ethical code by which the ombudsperson operates
- Multiple ways to contact the ombudsperson (email, walk-in, phone)
- A description of the types of reasons why employees might use the program
- A description of what the ombudsperson does to address those concerns
  - "The Ombuds will hear and discuss your concerns, identifying and evaluating options to resolve problems;
  - Opens avenues of communication and gathers information;
  - Serves as a neutral mediator to solve problems and resolve conflict, striving for fairness, equitable solutions and adherence to university policies;
  - Provides information about University policies and refers you to other university services and programs."

Design, Implementation, and Maintenance
Use of an ombudsperson method depends primarily on two critical factors: the selection of the ombudsperson(s) and the delineation of how the ombudsperson(s) will operate in your organization.

- *Selection of ombudsperson.* There is perhaps no specialist within your conflict management system who must have a wider array of skills, abilities, and knowledge than an ombudsperson.[6] For an ombudsperson, interpersonal, communication, conflict resolution, and diplomacy skills are absolutely paramount. Carefully constructed assessments can be used to assess these critical skills in job applicants. In addition, there are several professional ombudsperson associations that may provide useful resources.[7]
- *How an ombudsperson will operate in your organization.* There are a number of logistical issues that need to be addressed, such as
  - *How will the ombudsperson learn about a workplace issue?* There are various means by which employees could communicate mistreatment including anonymous hotlines and face-to-face meetings. It is important to include multiple avenues to reach an ombudsperson, because employees will vary in their preference and willingness to use certain avenues.
  - *How will the ombudsperson's performance be evaluated?* This is an important issue to consider upfront because most of what the ombudsperson will do will need to remain confidential. Your organization might consider providing systematic yet confidential feedback mechanisms. For example, we know one organization which uses online surveys (linked to the ombudsperson website). Respondents can complete a confidential survey online or print it out and turn it into a secure box. In addition, this organization includes questions about employees' experience with the ombudsperson within its yearly attitude survey.

Benefits
The cost savings achieved by using ombudspersons are well-documented. For example, one study conducted by the Ombudsman Association showed the use of ombudspersons is related to lower

turnover, less litigation against the organization, and even less work-place violence.[8] A good ombudsperson can effectively maximize the conflict management resources available to employees by communicating what is available and explaining their relevance to the particular situation. Also, ombudspersons can provide a critical role in preventing future mistreatment by advocating for systematic changes in policies or procedures.

Drawbacks
A potential disadvantage is that it may be difficult to establish the reputation of the ombudsperson. That is, employees may be particularly concerned about his or her links to management. Also, it may be difficult, in terms of financial resources, to have dedicated resources for this position.

Multi-Step Appeal Systems

Another option for your organization is a multi-step appeal system, commonly referred to as a grievance system. This is a very popular, formal, non-consensual method for addressing mistreatment in the workplace. Originally touted by unions as a way for union members to "voice" problems with management while being protected from retaliation, these systems were often used as a union organizing tool. Today nearly all union settings have a multi-step appeal process. Also more and more non-union organizations incorporate these systems to address complaints in their organization and possibly minimize the threat of unionization.

These systems are roughly similar to the US court system in several respects:

- The mistreated employee presents his or her situation (case) at the lowest level first.
- A person not involved in the dispute makes a decision about the situation.
- The decisions at each level can be appealed to the next highest level.

Example:
Sample Non-union Grievance Procedure

Step 1. A written appeal is filed with the mistreated employee's immediate supervisor.
Step 2. A written appeal is filed with the supervisor's manager.
Step 3. A written appeal is filed with the VP of Human Resources.
Step 4. Written appeal is filed with the CEO.

The appeal systems vary considerably across organizations both in terms of the number and nature of the steps. Here, the variety of ways by which organizations set up their steps will be discussed, followed by a discussion of how you can design a multi-step appeal system for your organization.

Initial Steps

Nearly all multi-step appeal systems start, in some shape or form, with informal discussion (as described at the beginning of this chapter). Typically, that is, parties are encouraged to discuss the issue informally with each other before initiating the appeal system. Informal discussion would thus serve as a "pre-step" for the grievance procedure – something that should be attempted before filing a grievance.

Example:
Informal Discussion as a Pre-Step in Grievance Procedure

Illinois State University identifies informal discussion as a desirable pre-step for its staff.[9]

Informal discussion of issues that can result in the elimination of misunderstandings and the resolution of disputes in a way that helps maintain the collegial atmosphere is preferable to the formal grievance procedures.

Another version of informal discussion in a multi-step appeal process is for the mistreated employee to present his or her case to the immediate supervisor who is then responsible for conducting a review or holding a hearing with both parties. The supervisor often serves as an informal mediator in this first step. However, this approach would not be appropriate if the supervisor is considered by the individual to be the source of the mistreatment.

Example:
Informal Discussion as First Step

The Oklahoma Department of Human Services identifies informal discussion as the first step of its grievance procedure. Below is an excerpt from the online manual.[10]

"Step one - informal discussion.

(1)   The purpose of the informal discussion is to provide the employee and the immediate supervisor, reviewing supervisor, or other person with authority to resolve the dispute the opportunity to address and resolve concerns and complaints at the lowest possible level. The effort to resolve disputes at this level may include, but is not limited to, the use of mediation. [DHS:2-1-168 through DHS:2-1-169]

(2)   An employee who has a grievable issue promptly brings the dispute to the attention of the immediate supervisor, reviewing supervisor, or other person who has authority to resolve the dispute and all parties strive to resolve the dispute.

(3)   If the supervisor is unable to resolve the dispute because it is not within his or her control or authority, the supervisor attempts to determine who can resolve the dispute and gives that person an opportunity to resolve the dispute informally or advises the grievant to proceed with filing the formal grievance, Form P-11 (new Form 11PE011E), OKDHS Grievance Form."

The main difference between a stand-alone informal discussion and its use in a multi-step appeal system is that in the latter context it may change the dynamics of the discussion. In particular, the parties would be aware that if they do not reach a resolution on their own:

- Then it will be decided by someone else in the next step.
- Then it is less likely they will be able to keep the issue private and it will become known to other organizational members.

As a result, someone who feels that they either do not have a good case or that knowledge of the situation would be particularly damaging to them may be more motivated to resolve the situation, and perhaps make more concessions, through Informal Discussion.

Middle Steps

If the initial steps did not result in a successful resolution, or if either side would like to appeal a decision that was made, then the next step is initiated. There are typically one to four middle steps in a multi-step appeal system. That is, the number of intervening steps in the multi-step appeal system varies between organizations and organizations also vary in terms of which steps they include. There are, however, common middle steps:

Example:
Appeal System Middle Steps

- Higher-level managers such as the Divisional or Facility Manager review the situation and render a decision
- Human Resources personnel review the situation and render a decision
- Higher-level managers review the situation and render a decision
  - E.g., Department Managers, Divisional Managers, Business Unit Managers, or Facility Manager
  - Human Resources Employee Relations Officer or
  - Vice President of Human Resources
- A review board or panel reviews the situation
  - E.g., a panel of peers, a panel of managers from various units, or a panel of peers and managers

---

Typically these middle steps are ordered in terms of the chain of command or in terms of the number of people serving as decision-makers for any given step.

The Final Step

You should give particularly careful attention to determining the final step in your multi-step appeal system. Again, there are a variety of final steps in use today, each with their own unique qualities and drawbacks. Sometimes organizations use different "final" steps depending on the nature of the mistreatment. For example, claims of discrimination or wrongful discharge have a statutory component and might be directed to arbitration (to be discussed later). On the other hand, claims of general unfairness, incivility, or misapplication of a policy might go to a peer review panel.

Peer review panel

One popular approach is the use of a peer review panel as the final step, although it is important to note that some organizations use it as a stand-alone process as well. Originated at General Electric in the early 1980s by Harvey Caras, a peer review panel consists of a number of employees who are selected and trained to serve in this capacity, in addition to their regular job duties. Usually a panel consists of 5 people; typically at least 3 of them are non-management. An organization might have one peer review panel that is used for all grievances or may have a pool of qualified peers who are randomly selected for any given grievance. Those who serve on peer review panels usually undergo training to become eligible. Often organizations have a policy which allows certain peers to be recused if they have a conflict of interest. The peer review panel would be responsible for hearing the evidence and issuing a judgment. Typically the judgment is based on the majority, rather than a unanimous opinion.

There are some advantages and disadvantages to this approach. First, such an approach is essentially a "jury of peers" and this has been shown to be a desirable feature, particularly in blue-collar fields. Mistreated employees may be more willing to accept the final decision as opposed to one made by management. Given its popularity in union dispute resolution systems, some organizations (e.g., GE, Marriott, TRW) have implemented peer review panels to provide comparable coverage and possibly stem union organization attempts. However, there could be some forms of mistreatment that are too complex for peer review and would be better served by an expert in the field. Also, such an approach is time-consuming for the peers who serve and it may be difficult for them to juggle their regular job duties as well.

Examples:
Peer Review Panel

A number of organizations have used, or are currently using, peer review panels as part of their conflict management system, including Marriott Corporation. Marriott's CEO, Bill Marriott in discussing the peer review panel says "It's almost like a jury trial."[11] The following are some key components of Marriott's system as it was implemented in the early 1990s.[12]

- About 10–15% of Marriott employees are trained to serve on the panel.
- Employees wishing to pursue the peer review panel can pull six peer names (out of box), and select 3 of those for the panel. The employee then draws 4 names of managers, and selects 2 for the panel.
- The panel meets within 10 days of its creation to make a final, binding decision.

In its first years of adoption, Marriott reported a significant drop in external agency charges (e.g., EEOC) and very positive responses from employees.

Arbitration

Arbitration as a final step involves employing outside experts as the final decision-makers. As noted earlier, some organizations include an arbitration clause in the employment contract, which essentially waives an individual's right to pursue a claim through the court system. The American Arbitration Association defines arbitration as "the submission of a dispute to one or more impartial persons for a final and binding decision, known as an 'award.' Awards are made in writing and are generally final and binding on the parties in the case."[13] Like mediators, arbitrators typically have training, education, and experience specific to the area in which they make judgments.

Many arbitrators are attorneys. The organization may choose to contract with a few specific arbitrators or may continually select from an arbitration service (e.g., the American Arbitration Association) that can generate a list of qualified arbitrators for a particular type of issue.

There are several known benefits of using arbitration as the final step. First, using outside experts in the particular area allows claims that are legalistic in nature (e.g., discrimination, harassment, wrongful termination) to be heard. So an arbitration ruling can be binding (e.g., when used with an arbitration clause) and the courts have given great deference to these rulings. Second, as neutral outsiders with experience and training, arbitrators have not only been shown to be considered credible by employees, but the resulting decisions are generally evaluated as fair. Also, the use of arbitration reduces the risk of jury trials and the potentially large damage awards that have accompanied employment lawsuits.

Disadvantages of this approach include the cost of hiring an arbitrator (an hourly fee similar to attorney rates, $175–$500+ per hour) and additional costs such as administrative services. Another disadvantage is that, unlike the court system, such an approach typically means the organization and individual cannot appeal an arbitrator's decision. Also, there is a danger of employees perceiving arbitration as the employer's attempt to take away their legal rights.

Chief executive officer

As with open-door policies, the final decision-maker is sometimes the top executive in the organization. This would be unheard of in a union setting, but it might be appropriate for your organization, particularly if it is smaller or hierarchical in nature. An advantage of this is that the CEO would be familiar with the context and the organization's policies. Disadvantages include the general unavailability of most CEOs and whether this would be considered acceptable to most employees.

Design, Implementation, and Maintenance

Developing and implementing a multi-step appeal system requires that you address several critical issues.

☑ How many levels? Multi-step appeal systems generally have three or more levels. In deciding how many to have in your system you should take into account how important timeliness is relative to other factors, such as acceptance. For example, a small number of steps would allow any given complaint of mistreatment to be processed more quickly. However, it may do so at the expense of perceived fairness. On the other hand, the more quickly a mistreatment is addressed, the less costly the toll it would take. The organizational structure also plays a role here. For example, you would usually have fewer steps with flatter organizations.

☑ How much and what type of documentation? With respect to this question you are juggling multiple desiderata:
  • Accessibility (less documentation is more desirable because employees may be more willing to initiate a complaint if less documentation is required on their part). Some organizations have short forms which can be used or restrict the length of a narrative (e.g., to one page) for each party to the dispute.
  • Consistency (more documentation is desirable because it ensures the same steps are being followed across complaints)
  • Time (less documentation is more desirable because it has less of an impact on the parties' and the decision-makers' time)
  • Mitigation of legal responsibility (more documentation is desirable because you would be better able to defend yourself if the complaint went to litigation)

☑ How much representation? That is, at what point, if any, would you allow the mistreated employee and the responding party to bring a supporter along (e.g., coworker). In a union context, the union steward would be involved from the time the grievance is written. Allowing representation may help to present each side's view effectively. However, it also may serve to increase the "litigation-feel" of the process and limit privacy.

☑ How much regulation? Multi-step appeal systems vary in terms of how regulated the process is with respect to:

- The amount of time allowed for each step. We know several organizations which require appeals and responses be made within five business days (unless a delay is agreed to by both parties). However, there are others which allow appeals and responses to be made within 30 days.
- Whether and/or when outside witnesses are allowed to testify. The companies with whom we have worked generally allow witnesses to be contacted as part of an investigation at any step, but do not allow them to be called until the final step.

☑ How will you protect against retaliation? Many multi-step appeals include a statement in the policy that retaliation against those who use the system is expressly forbidden. However, forbidding retaliation is not the same as preventing retaliation! There are, however, several things you can do to help prevent or minimize retaliation (see discussion below).

☑ How much flexibility? Another question to address is whether you would like some inherent flexibility in the system. For example, if the mistreated employee wanted to skip the lower steps and go straight to arbitration, would that be allowable?

Benefits

Your organization would likely benefit in multiple ways by implementing a multi-step appeal system. First, researchers have demonstrated that organizations who implement such systems tend to have lower staff turnover than other organizations. Second, this system allows you to find out the specifics of a particular problem internally, rather than externally (litigation), allowing you to have the information you need to address the problem and hopefully prevent it from happening again. An internal complaint procedure has also been shown to mitigate legal responsibility for cases that are later litigated.

Drawbacks

Unfortunately, such systems have their drawbacks as well. Most notably, practitioners and researchers have identified a heightened risk of retaliation against employees who use these systems. This not only damages the individual employee, it also makes it less likely that others will be willing to use the procedure. This opens your company up to retaliation claims, particularly if the mistreated employee was claiming discrimination or whistle-blowing retaliation. Also, such systems are fairly expensive in that they require time away from work-related duties for a number of individuals (decision-makers and the disputing parties).

Tips	
Dos of Multi-Step Appeal Systems	*Don'ts of Multi-Step Appeal Systems*
• DO encourage informal discussion or some other consensual process as an initial or pre-step to using the appeal system • DO have a separate process for addressing retaliation claims • DO involve employees in the design of the appeal system	• DON'T implement a new appeal system without training all of the decision-makers • DON'T assume there will be no retaliation without having steps in place to prevent it

Hot-lines

Another option you can consider is the implementation of a hot-line. Typically hot-lines are toll-free numbers, which can be used by employees to report organizational wrong-doing (e.g., whistle-blowing) or other forms of mistreatment. The hot-line could be staffed, in which case the staff member would carefully question the phone caller to get the needed information. Or the hot-line could be set up to only take messages. Usually such hot-lines are anonymous, although you could allow employees to reveal their identify if they wish to do so.

The critical question is what do you do with the information after it is received? There are several ways that this information could be used to address mistreatment, such as:

• *Initiating a workplace investigation.* Suppose, for example, that an employee calls in to say that his manager is sexually harassing his coworkers, but they are afraid to report it. Your organization could then conduct a careful workplace investigation and take appropriate remedial measures if necessary.

- *Initiating reexamination of a policy.* Imagine that one of your employees called in to report that a reimbursement policy is vague in certain respects, resulting in inconsistency across managers in terms of what expenses can be reimbursed. The policy could be examined and modified accordingly with this new information.
- *Initiating implementation of a new policy.* Information gained from the hot-line may offer insight on a needed policy. As an example, a call regarding idiosyncrasies in a manager allowing some employees but not others to telecommute or in offering flexible scheduling might suggest your organization should draft a policy about whether such programs are available at your organization, to whom, and the logistics.
- *Initiating needed training.* Phone calls on the hot-line might indicate a general problem with incivility within a few departments. This information might be used in a training needs assessment and an appropriate training program could be developed.
- *Initiating ombudsperson intervention.* If an employee is willing to self-identify, information on the hot-line is often provided to an ombudsperson who can then initiate facilitating a successful resolution of the mistreatment.

Benefits

The hotline approach may be the most appropriate way to initiate resolving mistreatment for certain employees or in certain situations. Consider a situation in which a manager is abusive to employees. Those employees may be particularly uncomfortable with confronting that manager about the abuse or, if the manager has political power, with reporting the manager's behavior to others. That is, they may think it quite likely that their action would make the situation worse. However, reporting it anonymously may be less intimidating. Another advantage is that it can provide you with detailed information you might not otherwise receive, allowing you to address problems earlier.

Drawbacks

Yet, this approach has its disadvantages as well. It may be difficult to get enough information to address a problem, either because the callers are unwilling to give more information or because they leave an incomplete message. This method also has the potential for abuse. An employee could call in to purposely give false, inflammatory information to initiate a workplace investigation as either a joke or to be punitive. The anonymity of the system may lead callers to feel unaccountable for the information they provide.

Common Concerns across Dispute Resolution Systems

The stand-alone dispute resolution systems just discussed certainly vary from one another. However, they also share a few things in common, particularly these three topics:

• The importance of organizational justice principles
• The importance of conducting careful workplace investigations
• The importance of minimizing retaliation

Organizational Justice Concerns

The extent to which the disputing parties will respond positively to the dispute resolution system will depend to a large extent on how far organizational justice principles[14] are followed. Most of the principles of organizational justice have already been woven into the previous discussion of the stand-alone systems. However, it is important to articulate them apart from the individual systems in order to underscore their importance.

• *Outcome justice*: Certainly the final decision made by an external party or arrived at by the disputing parties is important. It is particularly important that the final outcome is based on accurate information and that steps were taken to ensure accuracy (including, for example, appropriate workplace investigations).

All too often, those who implement dispute resolution systems tend to focus on the fairness of the final decision. Yet, the perceived fairness of the procedures used and the quality of interpersonal treatment received is also very important to individuals who feel they have been mistreated. Thus, careful attention should be made to ensure:

- *Procedural justice*: The fairness of the procedures used to make the decision is also important. The most important characteristic is that both parties should have the opportunity to express their views. The process should be consistently applied across time and people, be free from bias (such as friendships, political power), and uphold ethical and moral standards.
- *Interactional justice*: This refers to quality of interpersonal treatment received and has two components, informational and interactional. Informationally, it is important that the parties are given a full explanation for how a decision was reached. Interactionally, it is important that the parties are treated with dignity and respect throughout the process.

Workplace Investigations

Workplace investigations are typically not stand-alone systems; however, they are often used as part of stand-alone systems. For example, some multi-step appeal systems require human resources to conduct an internal workplace investigation whenever an employee makes a complaint of any type of workplace mistreatment. Or some systems require peer review panels or managers to conduct such investigations. If your organization does require a workplace investigation, or the legal issues raised by such a complaint merit a workplace investigation, your investigations should be:

- ☑ *Expeditious.* Investigations should be initiated quickly after the initial complaint, and it should be a high priority for the investigator to complete the investigation in a timely manner (typically within 30 days).
- ☑ *Thorough.* On the other hand, speed should not be at the expense of thoroughness. The investigator(s) should question all relevant parties to the mistreatment and verify the parties' accounts of the situation.
- ☑ *Documented.* Documentation is critical. Without it, you cannot establish that a quality investigation took place and you would be unable to use this to defend your organization in litigation. Given the importance of the documentation, the information should be treated like other critical human resource information and should be backed-up in some form and also protected for privacy.

☑ *Fair and free from bias.* The investigator needs to remain open-minded throughout the investigation to ensure what information is gathered and how it is presented is as accurate as possible.

☑ *Confidential.* If at all possible, the investigator(s) should maintain the confidentiality of both the mistreated employee and the responding party. As an investigator, you should assume that both parties wish to remain with the organization and that maintaining confidentiality would go a long way toward preventing additional mistreatment and retaliation. Should confidentiality be accidentally breached or have to be breached, then the parties affected should be made aware of it.

Selecting and training investigators

Selecting the right person(s) to conduct workplace investigations and providing them with quality, ongoing training is paramount, particularly given the sensitive and potentially legal issues that may be under investigation (or uncovered through an investigation). Investigators should be selected for their interpersonal and communication skills as well as their ability to probe and analyze potentially complex and sensitive issues. The training should consist of initial training (includ-

---

Case in Point:
Creating Legal Problems through Workplace Investigation

Jack was investigating a claim of sexual harassment made by Michelle, a bank teller, against Pete, another bank teller. In conducting his investigation, Jack interviewed Pete (the alleged "harasser") prior to interviewing Michelle (the complainant). Following his investigation, Jack concluded Michelle's claim lacked validity. However, because of his failure to interview Michelle first, she accused Jack of not fully understanding the nature of her complaint and making up his mind about the validity of the complaint before the investigation was complete, and ultimately being biased against her. Michelle pursued the sexual harassment claim through external litigation. The workplace investigation was found to be inappropriate and did not mitigate the bank's responsibility. The bank was held liable for sexual harassment.

ing both the legal, human resource, and communication aspects) followed by yearly (or semi-annual) updates. The quality of workplace investigations has important implications for the credibility of your system to other employees. If your investigations are known to exacerbate workplace mistreatment rather than facilitate resolution, few employees would be willing to report mistreatment internally.

Minimizing Retaliation

A concern with any dispute resolution system is that employees who use it (or employees who are identified as the source of the mistreatment) will experience retaliation as a result of using the system to resolve or address mistreatment. Many organizations have "no retaliation policies" indicated in their documentation.

Example:
Typical No Retaliation Policy

"Members of this organization are prohibited against engaging in retaliation against individuals who file a complaint or participate in an internal investigation."

However, to minimize or prevent retaliation, you need to take a much more proactive stance. Below are some tips for minimizing retaliation through careful auditing.

Tips:
Steps to Minimize Retaliation

- Train employees and managers – include a discussion of what is retaliation and how it might occur
- Include a separate process for reporting retaliation should it occur – if an employee experiences retaliation when using the multi-step system, it is unlikely he or she would use this same system to report retaliation. Today organizations are providing a separate process (e.g., ombudsperson) for handling retaliation claims.

- Carefully check for changes in the personnel records of employees who make complaints compared to similar others who do not make complaints. In so doing, check for such signals as the following:
  ○ "Surprises" in the performance evaluations
  ○ Slower than expected promotions
  ○ Increased absences or tardiness

Good to Know:
Key Points

- There are a number of stand-alone dispute resolution systems that differ in terms of formality and consensuality, making them more (or less) appropriate for certain types of mistreatment, individuals, and organizations.
- Each type of dispute resolution system has its unique advantages and disadvantages.
- Each dispute resolution system requires careful design and development so that concerns about process, confidentiality, and protection from retaliation can be addressed.

- Regardless of which dispute resolution system is implemented, it is important to follow organizational justice principles.
- Quality workplace investigations are a critical component of an effective dispute resolution system.
- Careful steps should be taken to minimize retaliation for using dispute resolution systems.

Chapter 7

Contemporary Best Practices: State-of-the-Art Dispute Resolution Systems

If you were to design and implement a state-of-the-art dispute resolution system, your system would be broad, deep, and integrated. It would be broad because it would offer a wide variety of dispute resolution approaches varying in terms of both formality and consensuality. Thus, it would include formal, adjudicative procedures (e.g., a grievance procedure) for mistreatment such as discrimination or a contract violation that is more legalistic in nature, as well as less formal, consensual procedures (e.g., informal discussion). It would be deep because it would not just resolve any given incident of mistreatment but be carefully designed to minimize or prevent the occurrence of further mistreatment, of that same employee or of others, and to repair the relationship(s) between the mistreated employee and the other party or your organization. Finally, it would be fully integrated into the way your organization operates.

So how does a dispute resolution system do all these things? To create such a system you would need to incorporate several key characteristics including:

- ☑ multiple options
- ☑ nested collaboration
- ☑ system facilitation
- ☑ training
- ☑ accessibility
- ☑ flexibility

☑ communication
☑ integration with organizational culture and work practices

In this next section, these specific characteristics of the best systems in use today will be described so that you can understand how you can create such a system in your organization. Note that there is not a single one-size-fits-all, state-of-the-art system. Instead, state-of-the-art systems incorporate the key characteristics in a way that is consistent with the organization's culture and goals.

Multiple Options

In the previous section, critical aspects of several stand-alone dispute resolution systems were explained. As you read through the previous chapter, you may have been disheartened to see that there seemed not to be one "best" stand-alone dispute resolution method for all situations. Clearly, any given approach – no matter how carefully designed – has its drawbacks; no single approach addresses all the concerns. Of course, given the range of types of mistreatment and employee preferences, it is no surprise that one stand-alone method cannot meet the needs of all situations.

However, best evidence-based practice is to provide your employees with a *choice* of procedures to address mistreatment at work. In particular, it is critical to offer both formal, adjudicative approaches (sometimes referred to as "right-based") as well as more consensual approaches (sometimes referred to as "interest-based"). Doing so allows you to maximize the fit between the type of mistreatment, employee preferences, and available options. For example, a state-of-the-art system would look something like this:

Good to Know:
State-of-the-Art System Components

- Informal Discussion
  - Listed as preferred initial approach for mistreatment concerns
- Ombudsperson
  - available in person and through anonymous hotline

- Mediation
  - Trained peer mediators
  - Professional mediators available on request as needed
- Multi-step appeal system
  - First step is informal discussion
  - Employees can appeal to any higher step and may skip steps if so desired
  - Mediation is included as an option
  - Final Step is peer review panel

While designing and implementing multiple dispute resolution approaches may seem daunting and unnecessary, the likely benefits are compelling, particularly when the options are well-integrated and consistent with the organization's needs. Practitioners[1] and research-practitioners[2] have heralded the numerous benefits of an integrated multi-option approach to dispute resolution. Such benefits include:[3]

- Employees having the option to use appropriate voice methods for their situation.
- Employees being less likely to avoid conflict when they have multiple options.
- Increased opportunity to address underlying basis for the mistreatment.
- More positive attitudes toward conflict and the organization.

Nested Collaboration

Another key feature of a state-of-the-art dispute resolution system is the extent to which collaborative approaches are nested within it. That is, collaboration as a means to address mistreatment is available and encouraged at various points within the system. Collaborative approaches are those in which the parties have control over the resolution of the mistreatment and work together toward a mutually acceptable solution. These approaches include informal discussion, mediation, and to a certain extent, the use of ombudspersons. As noted earlier, such approaches have several desirable benefits including:

- More "buy-in" from the parties
- Higher satisfaction with the process

- Lower likelihood of retaliation against the claimant
- Being generally less expensive than other alternatives

Despite these desirable characteristics, these collaborative approaches are not necessarily the first method that employees think of using when they feel mistreated. Thus, it is important to make these approaches more salient to the parties and to continue to make them an option, even after other, less collaborative approaches are attempted.

Tips:
Making Available and Encouraging Collaboration

- Identify informal discussion as the preferred, initial method to be attempted. This should be communicated throughout the organization, including in new employee orientation, training, and the available materials that describe the dispute resolution procedures.
- Include collaborative approaches as a pre-step or a step in less collaborative approaches, such as multi-step appeal systems.
- Allow employees to attempt collaborative approaches (e.g., informal discussion, mediation) at any point of the mistreatment resolution.
- Create a pattern of practice in which the organization will suggest and/or agree to mediation before it is addressed in court.

System Facilitation

Increasing the number of options available to mistreated employees for resolving the mistreatment will also increase the complexity of the system, making it even more critical that you provide resources to facilitate its full utilization. One important aspect of facilitation takes the form of trained individuals who can provide an overview of the entire system, explain how it works, and articulate the differences among the various methods. We have found that companies vary in their level of system facilitation.

- *Minimum level.* At a minimum level you would want to be certain that there are individuals within HR who can provide relevant information to members of the organization.

- *Moderate level.* In addition to HR, it would be helpful to have first-level supervisors and managers trained on the system at a general level as well as in the differences among the dispute resolution options.
- *Highest level.* Ideally you would have one or more trained professionals who could not only describe the system in general, but could also troubleshoot with the mistreated employee to identify the key issues involved in the situation and explain how the various dispute resolution options might work to address those issues. This function would be best served by an organizational ombudsperson; however, it would be possible to hire (or contract with) individuals who have some, but not all the skills of an ombudsperson, to serve as system facilitators. Of course, there are several other added advantages of having an ombudsperson beyond knowledge of the other systems in place (e.g., he or she could serve as an informal mediator and engage in other dispute resolution efforts during this stage). Another alternative is to use employee advocates who could make some aspects of the system more accessible to certain employees. In union settings it is common for employee advocates to be elected (often on a full-time basis). However in non-union settings it is common for employee advocates to be identified through self- and peer nominations and selected through a screening process which usually involves employee representation. Not all employees would have the skills, or perceive they have the skills, to use all the resolution options available. An employee advocate, often a trained peer, could help a mistreated employee navigate the system by doing such things as engaging in sense-making with the employee, helping the employee articulate what it is he or she is concerned about or would like to have addressed, or helping an employee write a written grievance.

Training

For any dispute resolution system to work effectively, it is critical that you invest in training. In particular, you need to invest initially in communication and conflict resolution training for all current employees and then for new ones as they come on board. Individual employees who will be playing specific roles in the process would also need training for roles such as peer review panel members, peer mediators, and employee advocates. It would also be critical to train managers and supervisors on role-specific skills. For example, if you decided to include a multi-step appeal system in which a supervisor or manager makes a decision, then you would want to train them on that aspect.

An often overlooked area of training is follow-up or periodic training renewal. Employees who have and who have not been called upon to use their conflict skills will need "refresher" training to get them back on track or to update their information.

Communication

There is considerable evidence that employees often do not know that they have dispute resolution systems available to them at work. The best system is of little value if your employees do not know it is there! Communication of the system, including the full range of available options, is critical. This communication can take place in a number of ways and venues:

- *New Employee Orientation.* Introduction to the system options, policies, and procedures can be included as part of new employee orientation.
- *Written Documentation.* A written, easy-to-follow, description of the system would be very useful. This might be included in the employee handbook and/or as a stand-alone document. This information should also be included in your company's online portal for employees. Be certain to update your organization's search engine with relevant, similar terms so that employees can easily find the resources online.

Accessibility

Another desirable feature for a state-of-the-art dispute resolution system is that it should be accessible to all employees. For example, the system may be inaccessible to some employees (or at least perceived as such) due to language barriers or poor literacy. Such employees may not understand how to initiate a complaint through the multi-step appeal system or how to communicate with a manager regarding an issue. Training sessions and documentation about your dispute resolution system should be communicated in a way that employees throughout the organization can understand. For example, if you have employees who have literacy problems, you might use voice-recorded PowerPoint presentations (delivered by a computer system with speakers/headphone) along with visually supportive material (e.g., symbolic representations) to provide a description of the dispute resolution process or to provide training for using the system. Another issue is that the system must be compliant with the Americans with Disabilities Act (1990) and thus accessible to disabled employees. Accommodating employees with disabilities may involve providing assistive technology devices to enhance communication for individuals who might need it, such as the hearing impaired or visually impaired. Or, it may mean providing modifications to the current system as needed if, for example, employees have social anxiety and discussing an issue in front of panel review would be problematic for them.

Another aspect of accessibility is that mistreated employees should be able to initiate a resolution process through multiple avenues instead of being required to initiate through one particular gate. This should be taken into consideration in the design and development of the multiple options. Aggrieved employees should be able to initiate the process from wherever they are most comfortable, including through a supervisor/manager, human resources, the ombudsperson, and/or an employee advocate or union steward. Simply having one "gate keeper" is likely to hinder system usage. Any one employee may be more/less comfortable approaching a particular person (e.g., supervisor vs. ombudsperson) and accessibility promotes the feeling that the organization is indeed committed to addressing workplace mistreatment.

Flexibility

You will, no doubt, have some unanticipated mistreatment situations or mistreated employees who do not "fit" with the way the system was originally set up. For example, an employee may have particularly strong feelings against going in front of a peer review panel and may want to use an external arbitrator instead. We have found that the mark of a true, state-of-the-art system is its ability to be flexible, as needed, to accommodate unanticipated preferences or requests.

Yet flexibility in your system does not mean that you encourage use of ineffective dispute resolution methods, but rather that your system is not so rigid that it does not allow for special, perhaps unanticipated situations. Flexibility should also not lead to inconsistency within the system. The flexibility you provide to accommodate the preferences or needs of one employee ought to be made available to other employees in similar situations. Otherwise, you risk perceptions of favoritism or even discrimination in how you treat your employees. To that end, it might be wise to include a statement, such as "We recognize there may be unique situations that merit alternative or modified dispute resolution methods. Employees may propose the use of alternative methods in such circumstances by contacting XYZ."

Integration with Organization and Culture

A dispute resolution system that works effectively at one organization will not necessarily work well at your organization. It is therefore critical that the selection and design of methods in your system be

---

Tips:
Integration with Organization and Culture – Questions for Your Organization to Consider

- *How will our company "treat" people who use this system?* Will they be viewed as traitors or complainers? If so, your organizational culture may need to change to embrace conflict (see Chapters 3 and 4) or your system may need to focus on methods that allow confidential resolution.
- *Is there enough trust in our organization for employees to be willing to use the system?* Attempting to resolve mistreatment internally requires employees to trust that your organization will hold up its end of the bargain. Or, if it involves peer mediators or peer review panels, it requires that mistreated employees are comfortable trusting their peers. If there is a history of mistrust in your organization, your system may not be used until that mistrust is addressed.
- *Does your organization solicit voice in other ways?* That is, does your organization include employees in task forces or solicit their involvement and ideas through other means? If not, asking employees to "voice" mistreatment may be a hard sell.

---

based on careful consideration of how it would work in your specific environment. As noted earlier, soliciting voice during the design and development of a system is critical to its success. Before rolling out a new dispute resolution system, employees should have had ample opportunity to provide feedback, particularly with respect to how the system would work in your unique organizational environment. It would be particularly helpful to enable employees to provide *anonymous* feedback as they may be hesitant to speak up if they think doing so could affect their work relationships.

State-of-the-Art Systems for Smaller Organizations

As can be seen from the previous section, offering a carefully constructed, comprehensive dispute resolution system is certainly daunting to most organizations, however, the payback for such efforts and resources more than offsets this investment. Yet, is such a system feasible in all organizations, particularly those that are smaller? Though the previous recommendations for a state-of-the-art dispute resolution system are not exclusive to large organizations, several potential barriers exist when considering the design and implementation of such a system in a smaller organization such as:

- It may not be economically feasible to have a dedicated ombudsperson employed by the organization
- The smaller number of employees may make it more difficult to have enough peer mediators who would not have conflicts of interest and/or personal or ongoing professional relationships with the disputing parties
- It may be difficult to ensure confidentiality, which may serve to make some employees less willing to voice their mistreatment

Given these potential barriers, there are a number of modifications that can be used to make state-of-the-art systems feasible in your smaller organization.

Increase use of modified procedures and external resources
A small organization could still offer a variety of resolution options, but to be cost-effective it might be best to modify the options or offer them through an external source. Here are some examples of how to modify the dispute resolution options previously presented.

- *Ombudsperson Modification.* As noted earlier, it may not be feasible to hire an internal, dedicated ombudsperson. However, it may be possible to use the following approaches:
  - Employ an ombudsperson on a part-time basis. This would allow you to use an internal person, and you could use any "downtime" for dispute resolution training and/or to serve in another capacity within your organization.
  - Create a relationship with an external mediator/facilitator. One of the advantages of an ombudsperson is that he or she is familiar with the organization and can use this information to facilitate resolutions. Your organization could create a similar situation by contracting with a mediator (such as through the Professional Mediation Association or American Arbitration Association) to provide similar resources, as well as mediation, as needed. The mediator/facilitator could be provided with initial information about your organization, culture, policies, and procedures and would learn more about the inner workings of your organization as he or she mediates disputes.
- *Mediation Modification.* Relying on internal mediators (such as peer mediators) may not be feasible given the greater likelihood of conflicts of interest among employees in smaller organizations. External mediation may be a viable alternative.
  - There are a number of sources of external mediators including the associations mentioned above that could be used in lieu of training employees to be peer mediators.
  - In addition, with an emphasis on informal discussion (earlier point), your organization could have a reduced need for mediation, making the cost of an external mediator, for those situations that need it, more feasible.
- *Multi-Step Appeal Process Modification.* As noted earlier it may be difficult to create a peer review panel in which none of the members has a conflict of interest or some ongoing relationship with one of the parties. As a result you might consider the following modifications:
  - Drop the requirement that members can not have conflicts or relationships with the parties. Dropping this requirement may raise other fairness issues, but the use of confidential voting on the panel could ease some of them.
  - Operate with a smaller number of members on the peer review panel.

○ Set up the peer review panel much like a jury in a courtroom. That is, have a certain number of peers randomly selected from the roster of employees. Then allow each side to eliminate a certain number of names until a final, agreed upon set is reached.

Address concerns about confidentiality and privacy through flexibility
It may be extremely difficult to protect the identity of a mistreated employee who uses the dispute resolution system in smaller organizations. In fact, it may not be reasonable for any organization to assure complete confidentiality. Yet, it is critical that employees who feel mistreated pursue some way to address that mistreatment, and confidentiality is an important determinant of system usage. Because of this issue, in a small organization it may be especially important to be flexible and open to alternative ways to address or resolve the mistreatment. This would begin with offering multiple options for employees to choose from, but also ensuring that employees can voice any concerns or requests given a unique situation. One small organization we know built such flexibility into their system, as illustrated in the following example situation.

Case Scenario:
Building Flexibility into Your Small Organization's System

Robert, an employee at a small electronics store, had a situation in which he felt unfairly treated by his supervisor regarding his scheduled work hours. Robert indicated that he thought racism was a factor in the scheduling. Informal discussion with the supervisor and mediation (facilitated by the personnel administrator) were unsuccessful. Robert was unwilling to use the multistep appeal process because he did not want his coworkers to become aware of his dispute and specifically that he was instigating changes to the work schedule which would then adversely affect some of them. The solution was to bring in an external arbitrator (approved by both Robert and his supervisor) rather than going through the initial, internal steps. While there was financial cost to the organization, resolving the dispute internally, rather than through the external court system made it well worth it. In the end, scheduling changes were made, and coworkers were not aware that Robert had filed a complaint.

Increase emphasis on training and informal discussion
Most complaints of mistreatment get addressed through informal discussion. The likelihood that a mistreatment situation would get resolved through informal discussion is even greater when:

• Both parties have good communication skills and conflict resolution skills
• Employees focus on informal discussion as the first, and preferred, step to address mistreatment concerns.

This underscores the importance of providing periodic, appropriate training to ensure employees have the skills to resolve issues informally and training all employees to seek informal discussion resolutions. Such an investment has the added benefit that employees can use these skills in other aspects of their jobs beyond workplace disputes. For example, such skills would be extremely beneficial for customer service (e.g., dealing with irate customers) and for interacting with suppliers and distributors (e.g., negotiating terms of a contract).

Recognizing the Limitations of State-of-the-Art Dispute Resolution Systems

This chapter has focused on designing state-of-the-art dispute resolution systems. Yet, even with the best system in place and with the best intentions of those involved, some issues simply don't get resolved to everyone's satisfaction. As noted earlier, mistreatment is in the eye of the beholder, and an individual may continue to feel mistreated, even when others around him or her disagree. However, the *perception* of mistreatment is what ultimately drives the costs of mistreatment to both the individual and organization. Recognizing that some issues may not be fully addressed to all parties' satisfaction (or at least perceived as such), how can you go about minimizing the adverse reactions and behaviors of individuals and minimize the deleterious effects to your organization?

Fortunately, there are ways to minimize adverse reactions, while further enhancing the overall quality of your state-of-the-art dispute resolution system. A stream of research has demonstrated that even if an outcome is unfavorable, an employee will react less negatively if he or she believes the *process* used to arrive at the outcome was fair.[4] The importance of following procedural[5] and interactional justice principles throughout your dispute resolution system cannot be emphasized enough. In particular, employees should believe:

- ☑ they can express their views and feelings during the process (e.g., the culture supports the expression of views and the procedure allows for it)
- ☑ they were treated with dignity and respect throughout the process
- ☑ they were given a full explanation for how a decision was reached or why a procedure was used
- ☑ the process was applied consistently across time and people
- ☑ the process is free from bias (e.g., friendships between other parties, political influences)
- ☑ the outcome was based on accurate information (e.g., efforts were made to verify the validity of information)
- ☑ the process upheld ethical and moral standards

By following such principles, you can better ensure that individuals will react less negatively even if they feel a specific issue has not been fully resolved and/or the outcome was unfavorable toward them. Conversely, failure to uphold such principles will intensify the frustration and discontent, even adding ammunition to an employee's perceptions of mistreatment.

Case Scenario:
The Importance of Interactional and Procedural Justice

A large law firm on the east coast had an employee, a paralegal named Todd, who had filed three complaints under the law firm's internal dispute resolution procedure over the past five years. In all three complaints Todd had appealed to the highest level (the managing partner), and in all three instances the

Continued

complaint had not been decided in Todd's favor. Todd continued to disagree with the final decisions in the three complaints. Yet Todd continued to be a high performer and did not express an interest in working elsewhere.

With three complaints in the past five years, the law firm might have labeled Todd as a chronic complainer and not treated his complaints seriously. However, the law firm's dispute resolution procedure had several desirable qualities and was perceived as fair by employees, including Todd. For example, whenever a decision was made, at each step the deciding person(s) carefully and thoroughly explained the basis for their decision and continued to express respect for Todd's (differing) point of view. They were also careful to keep the process confidential and very few employees were aware of Todd's complaints. The law firm credits these qualities (both interactional and procedural justice components) for minimizing Todd's negative reactions to the outcome of his complaints.

Good to Know:
Key Points

- A state-of-the-art dispute resolution system is broad, deep, and integrated.
- Key characteristics of a state-of-the-art dispute resolution system include multiple options, nested collaboration, system facilitation, training, accessibility, flexibility, communication, and integration with your organization's culture.

- Smaller organizations may face several barriers to the design and implementation of a state-of-the-art system, but modifications can be made to make the system feasible.
- The use of and adherence to procedural and interactional justice principles will help to mitigate negative reactions to unresolved mistreatment.

Chapter 8

Evaluating, Modifying, and Learning from Dispute Resolution Systems

So, you have implemented a dispute resolution system in your organization. Now what? How do you know it is working effectively? How can you determine if your original goals for implementing the system are being met? How can your dispute resolution system help to improve your organization's functioning? In this chapter, we discuss the continuous cycle of evaluating and modifying your system. The key theme is that managing and resolving mistreatment is an on-going process for any organization.

Auditing Your Dispute Resolution System

After you have designed and implemented a system for addressing mistreatment in your workplace it is very important that you measure whether that system is working and continue to assess this over time. But how should you do that? The effectiveness of organizational dispute resolution systems can be measured in a number of ways and with a number of approaches. Some organizations have focused primarily on *organizational*-level information, such as:

- Usage rates of the system
- Turnover and absenteeism rates
- Litigation costs

Others have focused on *process* measures of the dispute resolution system such as:

- The average length of time between initial complaint and final resolution
- The number of methods or levels used to reach resolution
- Perceived fairness of the system as reported by all employees, regardless of experience with the system

Finally, others have specifically examined the *experience of employees* who have used the system. This approach would include such measures as:

- Users' ratings of their experience with the system overall and specific components
- Users' subsequent performance ratings, absences, and turnover

All of the above criteria tell you something about your system, but each provides you with different pieces of information and it is not always clear how to interpret that information. For example, is a high usage rate a sign that there is a problem with your system (because there are many incidents of mistreatment) or that it is effective (because people are willing to use it)? Low usage, for example, might suggest that you have an amicable workplace or it might mean that the culture is so contentious that employees don't feel comfortable (or perceive futility in) voicing mistreatment. Similarly, the fact that an issue is resolved quickly does not mean that it was resolved fairly or acceptably to the disputants. Accordingly, you will need to measure an array of factors/criteria to ensure you are getting a complete and accurate audit of your system's effectiveness.

In this section you will be introduced to the major ways you might audit the effectiveness of your system. Before deciding how you will monitor and evaluate your system's effectiveness, however, it is important to examine your initial goals (see Chapter 5). Depending on the goals you set for your system, some of the measures of achievement described here may not be of interest to your organization, or your organization may have unique goals that require different approaches.

Measurement of Goal: A System that Successfully Addresses Employee Mistreatment

This goal is best measured by gathering information (typically via a survey) from those who have actually used the system. This would include measuring a wide range of variables from both the mistreated employees as well as the responding party.

What to measure?
There are a number of measures you could collect. As with any survey, you would need to weigh the cost of a longer survey with more measures (which people may be less likely to respond to) against that of a shorter one with fewer measures (which will provide you with less information).

Tips:
Possible Measures (Mistreated Employees)

- A general description of the mistreatment.
  E.g., Please describe, in general terms, what the mistreatment was about (from a list or open-ended), e.g.,
  ◦ The fairness of an organizational policy
  ◦ Supervisor's interpretation of policy
  ◦ Supervisor's decision
  ◦ Interaction with a coworker
  ◦ Interaction with: _____
- A description of what methods were used.
  E.g., Please check which of the following internal methods you used in an effort to address the mistreatment:
  ◦ Informal discussion with the other party
  ◦ Calling the hot-line
  ◦ Consultation with an ombudsperson
  ◦ Consultation with another third-party (e.g., Human Resources, Employee Assistance)
  ◦ Seeking the assistance of a union representative, etc.
- A description of the final result.
  E.g., What was the final result (from a list or open-ended)?
  ◦ I gave up
  ◦ The other party and I worked out a solution.

Continued

- o A third party (e.g., arbitrator, peer panel) imposed a solution.
- o I am pursuing it through outside, legal venues
- Satisfaction with the system and the experience.
  E.g.: How satisfied were you with:
  - o The methods available to you to use to address the mistreatment?
  - o The methods you selected to address the mistreatment?
  - o The resources available to you to support you in the process?
  - o The final outcome of the mistreatment?
  E.g.: Perception that the issue has been addressed:
  - o Not addressed at all
  - o Somewhat addressed
  - o Fully addressed
- Post-mistreatment relationship.
  E.g., How would you describe your current working relationship with the other party?
  - o It is much better than it was before.
  - o It is a little better than it was before.
  - o It has returned to the way it was before.
  - o It is not as good as it was before.
  - o It is much worse than it was before.
- Would you recommend this system to other employees who feel mistreated?
- Do you have any suggestions for making the system stronger?
- Measures of organizational outcome
  E.g., intention to quit the job, job search behavior, work withdrawal measures, loyalty to the organization, general job satisfaction

Often, the respondents to the dispute are overlooked in the evaluation process. However, you would also want to collect feedback from the responding party, whether it be a supervisor/manager or coworker. For many employees, receiving a mistreatment complaint would be a source of mistreatment for them as well. Collecting measures from the responding party would allow you to evaluate whether your system adequately addresses both parties' concerns. Several of the measures identified above would be relevant, as well as some other areas.

Tips:
Possible Measures (Responding Party)

- General type of mistreatment (from a list or open-ended).
  E.g., Please describe, in general terms, what the issue was about (from a list or open-ended), e.g.,
  - The fairness of an organizational policy
  - Supervisor's interpretation of policy
  - Supervisor's decision
  - Interaction with a coworker
  - Interaction with: _____
- Satisfaction with the system/experience.
  E.g.: How satisfied were you with:
  - The methods available to address the issue?
  - The methods used to address the issue?
  - The resources available to you to support you in the process?
  - The final outcome of the issue?
- Based on your knowledge, what methods were used (check from a list)?
  E.g., Please check which of the following methods were used:
  - Informal discussion with the other party
  - Calling the hot-line
  - Consultation with an ombudsperson
  - Consultation with another third-party (e.g., Human Resources, Employee Assistance)
  - Seeking the assistance of a union representative, etc.
- A description of the final result.
  E.g., What was the final result (from a list or open-ended)?
  - Not addressed at all
  - Somewhat addressed
  - Fully addressed
- Post-mistreatment relationship.
  E.g., How would you describe your current working relationship with the other party?
  - It is much better than it was before.
  - It is a little better than it was before.
  - It has returned to the way it was before.
  - It is not as good as it was before.
  - It is much worse than it was before.
- Do you have any suggestions for making the system stronger?
- Organizational outcome measures.
  E.g., intention to quit the job, job search behavior, work-withdrawal measures, loyalty to the organization, general job satisfaction

How to measure?
Another important question to address is how you would collect these measures. Certainly, confidentiality is a critical concern to both parties and the idea of completing a survey may make them nervous about how it will be used.

- *Distribution of surveys.* There are three main ways you could reach your target respondents:
  1. Your organization could have the surveys available online with a link prominently displayed alongside the description of the dispute resolution system.
  2. Your organization could send surveys (online link or paper-and-pencil) to employees who participate in any formal part of the system for which there is documentation (e.g., external mediator, multi-step appeal). The disadvantage, of course, is you would not get feedback from those who resolved a mistreatment complaint through informal discussion.
  3. Your organization could collect this information as part of a larger employee opinion survey. That is, the questions could be nested in the survey, with an initial question as to whether they have used the system and/or experienced mistreatment in the last year.
- *Return of surveys.* Again, anonymity and confidentiality are paramount. You might, therefore, consider having the completed surveys returned to, and the data analyzed by, a neutral party, enhancing the likelihood the respondents would respond openly.
  1. Ombudsperson. If you have an ombudsperson, this might be a logical person to whom to have the surveys returned.
  2. Outside vendor. You could also have responses sent to an outside vendor who could also evaluate the results. This approach has been used successfully with other sensitive issues such as exit interviews.

Measurement of Goal: A System Perceived as Fair

As we know from the organizational justice literature, a system that is procedurally fair, creates distributively fair outcomes, and enjoys sound interactional justice principles is paramount for enhancing the likelihood that employees will use the system if they have cause to do so. Certainly, you would want to collect organizational fairness measures from those who have used the system (including mistreated employees and responding employees). However, another critical group that you should examine in order to assess progress toward this goal would be the non-users of the system. By doing so, you would potentially uncover information on why the system is *not* used as well as on whether the system would be used should an issue arise. Again, there are a number of potential measures you could collect from this important group.

Tips:
Possible Measures (All Potential Users)

- Awareness of the system. As noted earlier, the best dispute resolution system is of little value if employees are largely unaware of it.
  E.g., How familiar are you with the dispute resolution system?
  - I am not at all aware of it
  - I have a little knowledge of its existence
  - I am completely aware of it
  - I have used it before
- Having cause to use the system. You would want to be able to compare the perspectives of mistreated employees who have not used a dispute resolution system with those of employees who have used one, and again with those of employees who have not felt mistreated.
  E.g., In the past year, have you felt mistreated in the course of performing your job?
- If yes, did you use the organization's dispute resolution system for addressing the issue?
  - Yes
  - No (if no, why not)? E.g.,
    - Concerns about privacy, confidentiality, etc.
    - Concerns about retaliation
    - Didn't know how to use it
    - Didn't think the mistreatment was a big concern
- Perceptions of organizational justice. You should use established measures that assess the following components of organizational justice:[1]

Continued

- Distributive fairness (e.g., The outcomes of the system are justified, the outcomes seem appropriate)
- Procedural fairness (e.g., The procedures are free from bias; I am able to express my views and feelings through the procedures)
- Interactional fairness (e.g., The parties involved in dispute resolution are respectful, the explanations regarding the procedures are reasonable)

Measurement of Goal: A System that is Cost-Effective

Of course, another common goal is to have a system that is beneficial to your organization's bottom line in terms of:

- Reducing the costs of mistreatment, such as
  - Turnover, absenteeism
  - Work slow-downs
  - Litigation
- Operating efficiency
  - Mistreatment is addressed promptly, minimizing the work time lost
  - Less expensive and more effective methods are used as often as possible

Often this type of goal is measured by examining organizational-level measures.

Tips:
Possible Measures (Cost-Effectiveness)

- Turnover and absenteeism rates after the system is implemented, preferably in comparison to rates before the system was implemented
- Litigation costs including attorney fees, judgments, and negative publicity
- Productivity measures before and after implementation of the system
- Employee recruitment costs (controlling for other changes) before and after implementation of the system. This might

indicate whether the system is improving your organization's reputation.
- Costs associated with the new system
  - Training expenses
  - Internal dedicated staffing (e.g., ombudsperson salary)
  - Internal staff time devoted to carrying out the system (e.g., supervisors, managers, peer review panels, HR)
  - External staffing needs (e.g., mediators, arbitrators)

As noted earlier, more collaborative methods are generally the most cost-effective. Accordingly, another important question to ask is: are the mistreatment issues that could be addressed at the lower levels actually being addressed there? Input from those who administer the system could be especially helpful in evaluating this aspect of the system's effectiveness as well as in providing input for making improvements to the system.

Tips:
Possible Measures (System Administrators)

- How many mistreatment complaints were you involved in as a _____ (peer review panel, decision-maker, mediator)?
- Of those complaints, should any of them have been handled through informal discussion between the parties?
  - If yes, how many?
  - What prevented these parties from using informal discussion?
- What can be done to improve the efficiency and effectiveness of the system?

Measurement of Goal: A System that Handles a Broad Range of Issues and Constituents

Finally, for this goal you will want to examine the system in terms of who is using it and why they are using it. You could collect this type of mistreatment information from the users themselves, though it may be difficult to collect data about the users without raising concerns about anonymity. Another extremely valuable source of relevant data, if it is available to you, is an ombudsperson. Typically, ombudspersons can provide aggregate information regarding system usage.

Tips:
Possible Measures (Ombudspersons)

- The overall number of mistreatment issues initiated, broken down by the types of mistreatment
- The level at which the mistreatment issues were resolved
- The methods used to address the mistreatment
- The demographics (e.g., level of job, gender, ethnicity, age) of those who initiated use of the system
- The demographics (e.g., level of job, gender, ethnicity, age) of those who responded to a complaint
- Cross-tabulations of the demographics of those who used various methods within the system, broken down by type of mistreatment

---

These measures would be particularly useful for identifying general areas of concern, such as:

- an increase in a certain type of mistreatment, particularly with respect to demographic information.
- disproportionate lack of use of the system by a particular demographic group.

Case Scenario:
Hispanic Concerns Not Voiced

Data provided by an ombudsperson at a large agency revealed that Hispanics rarely initiated complaints through the dispute resolution system, despite the fact that Hispanics comprised 10% of the work force. The system was utilized much more frequently by African Americans and Caucasian employees. For example, last year, six complaints were filed by African Americans, four by Caucasians, two by Asians, but no complaints were filed by

Hispanic employees. Though this may indicate that the culture is positive for Hispanics, the Human Resource Manager was actually very concerned when she received this data. She also knew that the turnover rate for Hispanics was the highest at the company (25% annual turnover compared to 5% for other employee groups). Following up on this data via an employee survey revealed that Hispanics reported low fairness perceptions for many organizational practices (e.g., merit raise and promotion decisions) yet significant concerns about retaliation for voicing issues at the organization. The organization then implemented programs (e.g., supervisor training on employment decisions, communication of no-retaliation and other workplace policies in Spanish) aimed at promoting a more fair work environment for all.

Examining who uses the system and for what purposes would be helpful in evaluating not only whether the dispute resolution system is used for a wide variety of mistreatments and throughout the organization, it could also help identify problem areas that could be addressed to prevent mistreatment (or larger issues, such at lawsuits) in the future.

Using Voice Information to Modify Systems and Organizational Practices

The information you obtain from evaluating your dispute resolution system can be used to not only improve your system, but also to improve your organization's overall functioning. The most effective dispute resolution systems are those that are approached as a "work-in-progress," subject to changes and modifications as needed. The key, of course, is the extent to which your respondents (e.g., users, non-users) are candid and forthcoming in their feedback.

Who Should Review and Modify the System?

To make the most of this information, you would want to have procedures in place for periodically and thoroughly reviewing the feedback as well as for modifying the system accordingly. To that end, you would need both an evaluation taskforce and a modification taskforce.

1) An evaluation taskforce is a dedicated group of individuals, who periodically review the evaluation information and identify areas of concern to target. The composition of such a taskforce and how the taskforce would operate would vary considerably across organizations. It may be beneficial to have individuals who are familiar with the system, but are not responsible for administering it to help prevent bias and bring in a fresh perspective. Some likely candidates include:

- Human Resource Management professional(s)
- Director of Employee Training
- Administrator of the Employee Assistance Program
- Legal professional

In reviewing the feedback information, it would be especially important that these individuals treat the feedback information with the utmost confidence.

2) A modification taskforce is a group which examines the areas of concern and identifies strategies for addressing the areas of concern. This committee would likely include the members of the Evaluation Taskforce, plus those with conflict management expertise, typically those who administer the system. These additional members might include:

- Ombudsperson (if you have one)
- Peer review panel member(s)
- Peer Mediators
- System Facilitators
- Outside experts (e.g., mediators, arbitrators)

How Often Should the System be Reviewed?

It is important to implement a timetable for periodical review to ensure that the information from your system is indeed reviewed regularly. Many companies conduct reviews annually, but you may want to do this more often if significant changes in the system (e.g., new method added, ombudsperson staffing change) or the organization (e.g., restructuring, changes in employee benefits) are made.

What Will the Process Involve?

One of the primary reasons for collecting information from your various sources is to examine how well your dispute resolution system is addressing mistreatment concerns. In particular, your gathered data allows you to examine how particular approaches are working as well as how the system is perceived by your employees. In examining the data, your evaluation taskforce should look at both:

- Quantitative data (such as average ratings for each method, usage rates, breakdowns by demographics, cost figures)
- Qualitative data (such as open-ended responses to why/why not they used the system)

Together this information can be used to identify potential areas of concern for the modification taskforce.

Your modification taskforce should then examine the potential areas of concern, and how to address these concerns, taking into account:

- Qualitative data (relevant open-ended suggestions from respondents about how to improve the system, obstacles identified, etc.)
- Dispute resolution literature including "best practices"

This information is then used to determine what action (if any) to take to improve your system.

Modifying Your System

There are several areas of inquiry that the modification taskforce might pursue to modify your system. Again, this depends, to a certain extent, on its original goals.

Tips	
Questions to Consider	*Possible Remedies*
• Are non-users aware of the dispute resolution system?	○ If not, what can be done to address this? (e.g., increased communication venues)

Continued

- Are those who have reason to use the conflict management system, choosing to use the system?

  - If not, what obstacles are preventing this? (e.g., lack of awareness, lack of trust, unsure how to begin, not comfortable with skills)
  - How can these obstacles be addressed? (e.g., Increased communication, steps to improve confidentiality/privacy, training)

- Are most issues being handled at the lowest levels?

  - If not, what are the obstacles? (e.g., lack of skills, unwillingness, type of mistreatment)
  - How can these obstacles be addressed? (e.g., training, policy changes, discipline)

- In general, is there a particular type of mistreatment that could be addressed through the system, but is not?

  - If so, is the supervisor the obstacle? (e.g., incivility, disrespect, fear of retaliation)
      How can this obstacle be addressed? (e.g., adding a hotline, improved management training & selection, increased retaliation protection)
  - Are the procedures the obstacle? (e.g., not allowed to have a supporter with them).
      If so, consider modifying this requirement.
  - Are the decisions perceived as unfair or to be based on politics
      If so, consider increasing the use of external decision-makers

Consider the system method by method

- Are those who use _____ satisfied with respect to the:
  Fairness of the process?
  Fairness of the outcome?
  Way they were treated?

  ○ For example, if one procedure is seen as less fair (e.g., multi-step appeal system) . . . why? (e.g., inconsistent information given about the process)

    If so, consider re-training those who administer the system and clarifying written materials

- What is the demographic breakdown of those using this method:
  Mistreated employees?
  Responding parties?

  ○ For example, if a disproportionate number of men use the multi-step appeals process . . . why? (e.g., respondents mentioned gender bias in the outcome favoring men)

    If so, consider changing the demographic breakdown of the decision-makers in the appeals process and providing additional training.

- What is the breakdown in terms of general job categories of those using this method (e.g., exempt vs. non-exempt, white-collar vs. blue-collar)?

  ○ For example, if a disproportionate number of white-collar employees use the method . . . why? (e.g., inaccessible)

    If so, modify the training and other materials that explain the process.

- What is the demographic breakdown, in terms of type of mistreatment, who use each method? That is, is a particular group over or under-represented for a particular type of mistreatment?

  ○ For example, if a disproportionate number of junior employees do not use the informal discussion to address workplace incivility . . . why? (e.g., fear of retaliation)

    If so, provide further retaliation protection and/or introduce a hot-line.

In addition, information about the types of mistreatment raised through the dispute resolution system, as well as about those that occurred yet were not raised through the system is an excellent source for identifying issues that merit specific attention by your organization, ultimately allowing you to prevent future mistreatment. Certainly there are other valuable sources of information about organizational problems such as exit-interviews or general attitude surveys. However, this voice source has the potential to provide you with detailed information on problems as they occur. A few of the potential applications include:

- *Identify, correct, and possibly remove problem managers.* Research has shown that one of the most important benefits of auditing your dispute resolution system is that doing so allows you to identify managers who may be chronic (or significant) sources of mistreatment.[2] It is possible such identification could lead to successful correction of problem behaviors (as explained in the next paragraph) or it could lead to a staffing change.
- *Identifying training needs.* Depending on how you can or do break down the information, you could identify training needs for departments, levels of management, or even particular shifts. For example, suppose a number of mistreatment issues had to do with how tasks or duties are assigned. This might indicate a need for management training on fairness issues. Or, suppose a number of sexual harassment complaints were identified in a particular department. This might indicate the need for further training for a few individuals or maybe the entire department. Or, if there is not enough specific information available in the feedback, it might stimulate you to conduct a formal needs assessment.
- *Identifying changes to your selection system.* Some information may indicate there are problems with how your organization is selecting people for the job. That is, some types of mistreatment might be best prevented through carefully revised selection procedures. Consider mistreatment scenarios in which incompetence, such as job knowledge, is relevant. For example, suppose a human resource analyst made errors in the database such that some employees' seniority levels were listed as lower than they should be and those employees subsequently had lower bonuses. While this mistake could be identified as the result of an unintentional error rather

than a manager purposely under-rewarding his or her employees, it does highlight a potential selection problem, particularly if your organization's intent is to hire based on skills rather than to train skills. Indeed, recurring problems such as these might suggest your current selection procedure is not as effective as it could be. As another example, if a number of mistreatment issues involve interpersonal conflict among team/group members, you may want to reexamine how you assess team skills in the selection process or possibly involve the team members' in the process of staffing those teams.

- *Identifying improvements to your performance management system.* This information could also provide you with insight about how well performance is being managed in the organization. For example, personnel decisions (e.g., merit increases, promotions) that are inconsistent with employees' performance appraisal ratings might indicate an area of concern with the utility of your performance management system.
- *Identifying disciplinary areas.* Some types of mistreatment might indicate the need to reconsider your discipline system. For example, the feedback may show that there are some "loopholes" in the policy on what behavior is reported and to whom, or that your progressive discipline process is being used inconsistently across your organization. It may also indicate that enduring behavioral problems such as those related to tardiness or safety are not being addressed.

In sum, while you may learn a lot about your dispute resolution system through a careful audit and review, you may also learn a lot about your organizational policies and procedures, workplace practices, and culture.

Good to Know:
Key Points

- Managing and resolving mistreatment is an on-going process for your organization.
- After you have designed and implemented a system for addressing mistreatment in your workplace it is very important that you measure whether that system is working in your organization, and continue to assess this over time.

- The effectiveness of an organizational dispute resolution system can be measured in a number of ways and with a number of approaches. What you measure will depend on the goals for your organization's system.
- The information you obtain from evaluating your dispute resolution system can be used to not only improve your system, but also to improve your organization's overall functioning.

Chapter 9

Repairing or Addressing
the Disputants' Relationship

All too often, organizations' attention to a mistreatment issue stops as soon as any of the following occurs:

- The parties reach some resolution on their own (i.e., through informal discussion) or with someone else's assistance (e.g., a mediator).
- A final decision is reached about the merit of the mistreatment claim (e.g., by an arbitration ruling).
- One of the parties leaves the organization.

Yet, as research has consistently shown, reaching a resolution or an employee's departure is rarely the end of the mistreatment's effect on the parties and organization. To fully address mistreatment and prevent further problems, it is critical that you give careful attention to how your dispute resolution system will attend to the continuing working relationship among the relevant parties. In this chapter, we discuss how your organization, and the parties involved, can work toward repairing or addressing their post-mistreatment work relationships.

What Are the Continuing Concerns?

The costs of mistreatment may continue if attention is not given to the working relationship among the parties involved. The employee who felt mistreated may continue to experience a range of emotions after the mistreatment is addressed (regardless of its outcome) such as a sense of betrayal that it happened in the first place, anger about how it disrupted his or her life, fear of what it will be like to work with the other individual in the future, regret over how they behaved or did not behave during the resolution, or self-consciousness about how to act now. The responding party can similarly experience a wide range of emotions during and after the mistreatment has been addressed or put to rest.

These reactions and the associated costs are not limited to the parties to the dispute. Some employees likely witnessed or actually were involved in the events surrounding the experience, voicing, and resolution of mistreatment. In addition, mistreated employees and responding parties may also engage in further sense-making with coworkers during the process and after the mistreatment has been resolved. Many other employees may also be aware of some aspects of the situation by hearing it through the grapevine or by observing others. One particularly sticky problem that organizations and the individuals involved face is that, because dispute resolution processes often assure confidentiality (to the extent possible) and involved parties do not want information shared, employees are often left to draw their own conclusions about what happened and how it has been resolved. This means that coworkers and peers will be familiar in varying levels with the situation, will receive their information about what happened from varying perspectives, and are likely to have their own reactions as well. This lack of complete information or lack of balanced information can contribute to a "charged" environment which makes it even more difficult for the disputing parties.

What is most pressing about these reactions is how they can continue to negatively impact your organization even after the mistreatment is "resolved."

Good to Know:
Ongoing Concerns After the Mistreatment is Resolved

- Coworkers' reactions to their understanding of the dispute may negatively shape their interactions with the disputing parties.
- The disputing parties may not work together effectively.
  - One or both may be hesitant to raise task-related issues freely.
  - One or both may harbor anger or resentment toward the other.
- The experience with the mistreatment may affect how the mistreated employee (and the people with whom he or she sense-makes) perceive other situations in the organization.
  - Their perception of the situation will be relayed in future sense-making with others.
  - Their perception of the situation will influence interpretation of other policies, work practices, and decisions.
- Others who work with the disputing parties may be affected by the disputing parties' changed relationship.

A Spiral of Mistreatment

The ultimate post-treatment concern regarding a damaged working relationship is the threat of a downward spiral of mistreatment or perceived chronic mistreatment within your organization. While voicing and addressing a particular *incident* of mistreatment may be considered an individual success, failure to repair or address the working relationship may actually lead to further, perhaps even more significant mistreatment concerns. Indeed, some workplace violence literature[1] supports the idea of an "escalation of aggression," in that aggressive responses are typically the end result of an initial feeling of mistreatment that was voiced, but that the individual feels was not fully addressed, so that it ultimately spirals into more serious reactions.

Fortunately, there are things your organization and the parties involved can do to mitigate or circumvent damage to the working relationships. Here, you will learn how the post-mistreatment

Case Scenario:
A Spiral of Mistreatment

Todd, a manufacturing supervisor, filed an appeal against his facilities manager, Jessica, in the multi-step appeal system in regards to a disciplinary action. The issue was "resolved" with the assistance of a higher-level supervisor, but there was no discussion between Todd and Jessica about how they would move on after the process was complete. After the process, Jessica felt uncomfortable around Todd, and began to be "distant" and "cold" when interacting with him. For example, in department meetings, Jessica avoided making direct eye contact with Todd. Todd's coworkers noticed that Jessica appeared to be treating Todd differently and asked Todd what happened in regard to his use of the appeal system. Todd was unsure what he should say/not say, so he merely said "it's over." When Todd received a job assignment that he did not care for, instead of approaching Jessica to see if another task could be assigned, Todd assumed Jessica was retaliating against him. He became increasingly resentful and ended up complaining to coworkers. Todd's coworkers started to complain among themselves about Jessica's unfair treatment. Soon they started to make comments under their breath during meetings, laughing at each other's comments and sending hostile looks at Jessica. When Jessica asked what they were talking about, Todd lost his temper and started to shout at Jessica. An administrative assistant who was seated outside the meeting room called security.

relationships should be examined and addressed, to minimize damaging effects of the mistreatment and maximize potential positive outcomes.

Acknowledge the Elephant in the Room and Figure Out How to Get it Out of There!

One of the most important steps in your dispute resolution system is for those involved to acknowledge that the situation occurred and that it might change (temporarily or long-term) how people interact. Certainly it is tempting to "get back to normal" or pretend that it never happened. However, by ignoring the situation, the parties involved do not necessarily have the opportunity to address their working relationship. In addition, some parties may think everything will easily return to normal, when in fact they may have some unanticipated struggles down the road. For example, coworkers' reactions may exacerbate the situation.

How and with Whom?

So, how do the disputant parties acknowledge the "elephant in the room"? That is, how and with whom should this conversation take place? This depends, to a large extent, on how the issue was resolved and the nature of the perceived mistreatment.

Tips: Post-Discussion Mistreatment	
When to Use	*Method*
• When informal discussion was used	• Between the parties only
• When a collaborative method was used, but the issue was not addressed through informal discussion	• Both parties are present with a facilitator (e.g., ombudsperson, mediator, HR professional); parties have the opportunity to speak privately with the facilitator
• When a decision was imposed on the parties, when the issue was particularly contentious (in the eyes of those who participated), or when the complaint is related to statutory concerns	• Parties meet with a facilitator separately who then makes a recommendation to HR and may follow up with both parties in a joint meeting

The above table provides a rough guideline for how and with whom a conversation about the post-dispute relationship should take place. Flexibility is a key consideration: If one or both parties would like to have a facilitator involved, or would like separate meetings with the facilitator, then that request should be honored.

What Issues Should be Considered?

There are a number of issues that should be considered in such a post-mistreatment conversation. The most important is "how will this experience affect working relationships?" This requires a frank discussion, or analysis, of anticipated or potential problems the parties could experience after they resume their relationship once the issue has been resolved.

While we may all readily agree that this is the right thing to do, what can you do to make sure this happens in your organization? We work with one organization that has used several means to enhance the likelihood that such a conversation takes place. First, it specifically listed this as the last step of any dispute resolution option in the organization. That is, all the materials (e.g., website, employee handbook) include a statement that says something like this, "The last step of any resolution process is to engage in a discussion with all relevant parties about how addressing this dispute might affect the working relationships of those involved and what steps can be taken to enhance the working relationships." In addition this organization focuses on that particular issue in its manager training. Finally, as the

---

Case Scenario:
Acknowledging the Issues

In the previous example, Jessica and Todd did not acknowledge the elephant in the room, let alone have a frank discussion about what issues might arise after the multi-step appeal was complete. If they had done so, there were several issues they should have addressed, including:

- What would the two of them tell others who asked about what happened?
- How would each of them respond if others made derogatory or snide remarks about the other party?
- How would they resume their manager–employee relationship? (e.g., what aspects of the relationship would be awkward and how could the awkwardness be minimized?)
- How should Todd respond if he felt Jessica was retaliating against him?

dispute resolution system (in this case, a multiple appeal system) requires written documentation, the parties have to sign a statement that this conversation has taken place and provide a date for its occurrence.

The goal is also for the parties to reach some agreement about how they will explain what happened, if need be, to their coworkers or peers. It may not be possible to reach complete agreement on what to say to whom, but the parties may be able to agree on what they will *not* say. Or, the parties may agree not to discuss the matter with others in the workplace at all.

When to Have This Discussion?

In some situations, it would be appropriate to have this discussion at the end of the resolution, and thus incorporated as part of your system. For example, this discussion could naturally take place at the end of a successful informal discussion. It could also be a part of a mediation process (e.g., "where do we go from here?"). For some mistreatment resolutions, this discussion would need to take place in a separate sitting. For example, when a multi-step appeal process is used, it may take a while before the parties have decided to accept, rather than appeal, the decision. In this type of situation, a separate meeting or meetings would be needed and should be explicitly incorporated as part of the system. Regardless, it is important to incorporate as part of your dispute resolution system a process to examine and address the disputants' post-treatment relationship. All is not necessarily "back to normal" once the arbitrator has rendered a decision or equity has been restored.

Should Someone Be Moved?

Another important issue to consider is whether one or both parties should be transferred out of their current position to another one within the organization. Previous research has found that transfers help to minimize retaliation, particularly if the mistreatment complaint focused on the manager's actions. It would be very rare to choose this course of action, but it might be a prudent decision if the relationship is significantly damaged, if it is unlikely that it is reparable because one or both parties is unwilling to reconcile, or if retaliation seems likely. Of course this decision would need to be made in close consultation with Human Resources and others who have the authority to make the decision. However, it would be especially important to consider how this movement would be perceived by others in the department. That is, would moving the manager suggest the manager did something wrong? Similarly, would moving the employee suggest that if you complain you get moved? Related to this, it is important that the transfer is not seen as retaliation against the mistreated employee. For example, changes in job duties, departments, even locations can be viewed by an employee (or others) as a "demotion" and thus subject to retaliatory claims. Careful consideration, including the solicitation of feedback from the parties as appropriate, should be paid to how personnel decisions will be interpreted and, when possible, the reasons for movement should be explained.

Communicating with Coworkers

Though ideally the conversation between the parties takes place before they share information with others so that everyone receives the same message, it is likely that those involved have discussed matters with someone. Depending on how many people know about the situation, it may be best for the manager (assuming he or she is not involved) to "clear the air" by announcing whatever information or explanation was agreed to and emphasizing the importance of allowing the parties their confidentiality. It will also be important for the manager to keep a finger on the pulse of the workgroup to stay alert to possible gossip or misperceptions. This will allow the manager to stay ahead of and act upon developing issues.

Moving Forward

In most situations, the working relationship can continue. It may take little or no repair or it may require a considerable amount of concerted effort to reconcile. In this section, you will learn about the range of ways by which an organization can help to repair a working relationship after mistreatment has occurred.

Awareness and Monitoring

In many cases, disputants simply having an open discussion about their working relationship can serve to address awkwardness or uncertainty in the post-mistreatment relationship. That is, simply identifying the "elephant in the room" can help ease concerns and open up communication lines about the relationship. If this is the case, the awareness can serve to motivate and ease relationship repair. It may also be helpful to plan one or two follow-up opportunities where the parties address any ensuing concerns about the post-mistreatment relationship and stem any misunderstandings from spiraling into future claims of mistreatment.

Repairing the Relationship

In other situations it may require more concerted effort to restore or reconcile the working relationship. As the practice and research literature in clinical psychology and marriage and family counseling attests, *how* to repair a relationship is not always so clear, and all efforts are not necessarily met with success.

Although relationships may have been viewed historically as the purview of clinical psychologists and related fields, today I-O psychologists and other researchers have started to examine the restoration of relationships at work. In particular, psychologists have examined relationships after some kinds of mistreatment such as sexual harassment or broken promises have occurred. In this section, we discuss the major concepts that are being examined to provide you with the background and vocabulary. However, this area is not yet at the stage that lends itself to a "how to" description. Indeed, if anything, it underscores the need to consider the restoration of relationships at work carefully, and the importance of clinical and counseling expertise in implementing any solution in difficult situations.

There are several related constructs concepts that have been investigated in this area including:

1. forgiveness
2. reconciliation
3. trust
4. restorative justice

In this section you will learn about these four concepts and the possible implications for relationship repair in the workplace. One important question for you to address, however, is who should be involved in the relationship repair process? Given the nature of the skills required, it would be particularly helpful to have someone with expertise in counseling (e.g., a clinical psychologist), and particular expertise with work relationships, especially when situations require more reparative work.

Forgiveness
The concept of forgiveness is a popular topic of study in a number of disciplines (e.g., law, philosophy, religion, psychology, management) and there are varying, but related definitions of it. For our purposes, consider the two definitions below.

Good to Know:
Forgiveness

- *Forgiveness Definition A*: "a process by which an offended worker cognitively acknowledges the wrongfulness of an injurious act and deliberately chooses to release negative emotions and inhibit the desire for revenge."[2]

- *Forgiveness Definition B*: "a conscious decision – while acknowledging the seriousness of the wrong – to release or forego bitterness or vengeance."[3]

In both definitions, an individual is choosing to consciously suspend or neutralize whatever negative feelings he or she may have about the mistreatment issue. Some definitions go farther to say that the negative feelings are replaced with a positive regard for the other party as well. However, it is important to note that forgiveness is not:

- Forgetting about what happened
- Condoning the behavior
- Excusing the behavior

Certainly, forgiveness from either or both parties would have desirable consequences for the individual as well as your organization. Research has demonstrated that forgiveness is linked to better mental health (e.g., less anxiety, reduced depression, less anger, higher self-esteem) and physical health (e.g., blood pressure, cardiovascular health). These benefits directly link to your organization's bottom-line by reduced absences and health benefit costs.

However, what is perhaps most beneficial is that reducing the negative emotions surrounding the mistreatment through forgiveness will help to reduce the likelihood of chronic perceptions of mistreatment. That is, releasing these negative emotions may prevent a one-time occurrence of mistreatment from shaping or cultivating future perceptions of mistreatment, as noted earlier in the discussion of the spiral of mistreatment.

A logical question to ask is: how can you enhance the likelihood that the parties will forgive one another? Unfortunately, the answer to that question is not very straightforward and a full answer is beyond the scope of the book. However, there are several relevant sources that speak to that issue.[4]

Clearly, forgiveness is a positive outcome in and of itself, but how does it fit in with the process of restoring a work relationship? One important thing to keep in mind is that forgiveness does not necessarily lead to reconciliation. That is, an employee may be able to release the bitterness or anger over a mistreatment, but may not be interested in repairing a work relationship with whoever caused the mistreatment, let alone be willing to trust the other person again. However, the next two concepts, reconciliation and rebuilding trust, are related to this idea.

Reconciliation
Reconciliation is, of course, what you hope will happen after a mistreatment issue is settled. That is, both parties will be willing to work at restoring the relationship.

Good to Know:
Reconciliation

- "Reconciliation is realized when both parties exert effort to assist in rebuilding a damaged relationship, and it connotes a desire to settle issues that led to the disruption of the relationship so the relationship can be restored to vitality."[5]

But what makes it more likely that the parties will make these efforts at reconciliation? Research in this area is limited; however, empirical research has found the following factors to be related to someone being more willing to reconcile in a business relationship:

- ☑ When the other party actually apologizes and gives an explanation.
- ☑ When the other party takes ownership of the mistreatment.
- ☑ When the apology occurs in a timely manner.
- ☑ When the apology seems sincere.
- ☑ When the parties previously enjoyed a good relationship, particularly when the mistreatment is severe.
- ☑ When it seems unlikely that the mistreatment will be repeated.

Though it's r eally up to the involved parties to take these steps, we know from best practices there are some general ways in which you can help the involved parties reconcile.

Tips	
Dos	*Don'ts*
• DO encourage parties who feel remorse to offer a sincere apology to the other party (in private). • DO take steps to enhance the fairness of your HR policies and workplace procedures.	• DON'T demand or require that one party apologize to the other. Sincerity is key, and a false apology could cause greater problems.

There is some evidence that establishing a "fair" workplace more generally can help facilitate reconciliation between disputing parties. In particular, research has also found that mistreated employees were more willing to reconcile when they perceived a positive procedural justice climate[6] in terms of the fairness of procedures such as:

- Promotion and pay raises
- Employee discipline procedures, including termination
- Performance appraisal procedures

Trust

If both parties are willing to reconcile and work toward repairing their work relationship, this opens up the door for rebuilding trust between the parties. Rebuilding trust is paramount to an effective working relationship. That is, "effective organizational functioning necessitates the presence of trust due to the impracticality of contracting all aspects of working relationships."[7]

Good to Know:
What is Trust?

According to Denise Rousseau, Sim Sitkin, Ronald Burt, and Colin Camerer trust is "the willingness to accept vulnerability based upon positive expectations about another's behavior."[8]

If the parties are willing to reconcile, how can they then rebuild their trust in one another? Key factors to repairing trust within a relationship include:[9]

- If the mistreatment involved deception (intentionally giving false information), it is less likely that trust can be restored.
- A promise (about future behavior) can help with initial trust repair.
- Consistent, trustworthy behavior helps most with trust repair, particularly over time.

As noted earlier with the discussion on reconciliation, a sincere apology between the disputants can be helpful in initiating trust repair. But, what can you do to enhance trust repair after a mistreatment situation occurs between employees? While words can help start the repair process, it is actions and behaviors that really drive the trust repair.

| **Tips:** |
| **Trust Repair** |

☑ Identify what behaviors/actions led to the mistreatment, specifically those that were identified through the dispute resolution system as being problematic and in need of remediation.
☑ Identify what would be needed to change those behaviors/actions (e.g., training, feedback).
☑ Consider creating a promise agreement that identifies what steps would be taken to change the behaviors/actions.
☑ Provide resources to support changing behaviors/actions.
☑ Follow up to give feedback about progress.

Restorative justice
Restorative justice is another concept to consider in repairing relationships. It was first developed in the criminal behavior domain (restitution to the "victim" from the "offender"), but is now applied more broadly to encompass constructive and peaceful approaches to restorative resolutions for wrongdoing in our communities. The key is discipline with support.

| **Good to Know:** |
| The Theory of Restorative Justice |

Restorative justice is a theory of justice that engages those that are harmed and the wrongdoers (and the community, where applicable) "in search of solutions that promote repair, reconciliation, and the rebuilding of relationships."[10] According to the Center for Restorative Justice at Suffolk University, restorative justice is based on the values of:

☑ inclusion
☑ democracy
☑ responsibility
☑ reparation
☑ safety
☑ healing
☑ reintegration
☑ respect

Restorative justice includes the following processes:

- Parties involved are given the opportunity to express their views of the situation and the impact on them personally
- Remaining questions are brought forward and answered
- The offending party "compensates" the victim
- A plan for prevention of future issues is developed through participative problem-solving
- The offending party is held accountable for adherence to the plan

Clearly, the above processes are most applicable in the context of criminal cases and human rights violations. Indeed, most of what we know about restorative justice comes from the justice system rather than the workplace. However, adaptation to the workplace context is nascent, but clearly feasible. In particular, some organizations are starting to use restorative justice principles in sexual harassment situations.

Case Scenario:
Restorative Justice in the Workplace

Patty has recently hired David as an assistant for the program development office she manages at a small non-profit organization. One of Patty's colleagues, Ann, knows David through mutual friends. Ann is very unhappy that David was hired. She does not like David primarily because of some issues she has with his religion. In the week leading up to David's start date, Ann proceeds to say negative things about David and his religion to coworkers and also acts rudely toward Patty. By the time David has arrived, most of his coworkers have heard about Ann's concerns and Patty has heard them as well. Several people make references to David about his religious beliefs, even though he has never talked about his beliefs at work. After being excluded from some after-work socializing and not being on the distribution list for several work-related emails, David begins to feel as though he is being discriminated against by his coworkers for his religious beliefs.

David decides to approach his manager, Patty, about this concern because informal discussion with the immediate supervisor is listed as the first step of the non-profit's dispute resolution process. After Patty and David talk, they decide it would be best

Continued

to meet with Patty's manager, Marvin, in part because Patty feels she has been the recipient of Ann's behavior as well. Marvin had also heard rumors of Ann's concerns and the way she approached the situation (by gossiping and acting rudely).

Marvin conducts an investigation where he learns more specifics about what Ann has said to others. He calls David and Ann into his office for a meeting. During the meeting, David and Ann are given the opportunity to express their views and concerns. In the course of the discussion, particularly after seeing David's reaction to learning what she has said, Ann admits that what she has done is unprofessional, disrespectful and intolerant. The conversation becomes emotional as Ann expresses her regret for how she handled the situation. Marvin encourages Ann to apologize to David, Patty and others whom she made feel uncomfortable. He also emphasizes that discrimination or treating someone poorly because of their personal values, including David's religious beliefs, is unacceptable and will not be tolerated. Marvin suggests that Ann spend some more time thinking about how the situation (David's coworkers not fully accepting him) could be rectified.

The three meet again the following week where Ann reveals she would like to do some further study on David's religion and that she wants to make it right by apologizing to the people with whom she spoke and share what she has learned. David accepts this solution and the three of them agree to meet again in several weeks to evaluate the situation again.

Unsuccessful Relationship Repair

Sometimes, relationships that were originally believed to be reparable turn out to not be so. As noted earlier, this may mean that removing an employee from the situation or making some other change to facilitate effective functioning of the workgroup (e.g., change in reporting structure, job duty reassignment) is necessary. It is important that any such action should not be seen as retaliation against an individual, as retaliation would likely stifle employees from voicing concerns in the future and could also be illegal if the initial claim of mistreatment falls under legislative protection (e.g., Title VII, Whistleblower Protection Act). However, in situations where there is no foreseeable resolution to the working relationship, it may be best to separate the employee from the situation and/or other individuals involved. Simply ignoring the situation, in hopes that it will get better is unlikely to be an effective strategy; taking action to separate the "problems" may be the only way to restore effective workgroup relations.

Good to Know:
Key Points

- After the mistreatment is addressed or the system has been exhausted, it is critical to consider the continuing effects of the claim of mistreatment on the individuals involved (the claimant, coworkers, and the one who might have been blamed) and their working relationships with one another.
- Without proper attention to post-mistreatment work relationships there is a continued threat of a spiral of mistreatment and even more adverse reactions.

- One key step to addressing the post-mistreatment work relationship is to have a discussion about it with the relevant parties.
- Sometimes additional effort and professional expertise is needed to help repair the relationship using principles related to forgiveness, trust, reconciliation, and restorative justice.

Chapter 10

Mistreatment Prevention and Resolution – The Big Picture

A s the popular media, practitioner literature, and research literature will attest, preventing and resolving mistreatment in the
workplace has become a critical concern to organizations. In this
book we have focused on how you can minimize the likelihood of
mistreatment occurring in your organization through preventive
measures, by better understanding how individuals arrive at conclusions of mistreatment and by fully addressing mistreatment in your
workplace when it does occur. In this concluding chapter we highlight the overarching themes in the book.

The Many Aliases of Mistreatment

There are a number of aliases for what we define as mistreatment in
the workplace: "when an employee believes that he or she has not
been treated fairly in the course of performing his or her job." Some
aliases or mistreatment terms have been discussed as stand-alone
topics in the media, practice, and research literature. For example,
incivility, bullying, harassment, discrimination, and retaliation have
all been given a considerable amount of attention recently. Likewise,
the fairness of outcomes received (e.g., pay raises) and the fairness of
the procedures used to make decisions (e.g., voice) have been subject
to scrutiny over a long period of time.

While the types of mistreatment mentioned above may vary in
terms of such characteristics as severity or legality, they share one

overriding thing in common: all focus on an employee feeling unfairly treated at work in some way. Given the plethora of specific types of mistreatment being discussed and examined today, it is particularly important to understand that research and practice have shown that the ways in which individuals evaluate potential forms of mistreatment and react to mistreatment are overwhelmingly similar.

The Importance of Sense-Making

Two individuals experience a similar incident with their supervisors; one concludes he has been mistreated, yet the other does not. How do individuals derive meaning from situations in such a way as to reach different conclusions about a similar experience? Individuals make sense of a situation through examination, discussion, reflection, and analyses. An individual is likely to engage others such as friends, family members, and coworkers in this process, and their perspectives and suggestions will influence the individual's interpretation of the situation and ultimately his or her conclusion that mistreatment has taken place (or not).

Given that the ultimate outcome of the sense-making process is a conclusion of mistreatment (or not), this process clearly sets the stage for an individual's subsequent psychological and behavioral reactions. Yet the effects of the sense-making process go beyond the specific incident in question. As others learn about, process, and evaluate the present situation, their perceptions of other situations (including future situations) and of the people involved in them are shaped. The key take-away here is that *an instance of "potential mistreatment" does not occur in a vacuum, but rather it is influenced by, and influences, the way that the individual interprets other experiences as well as the way those with whom he or she engages in the sense-making process interpret them.*

Costs of Mistreatment

All too often the costs of mistreatment are identified in terms of attorney fees, settlements, or court awards. Yet the toll of mistreatment in the workplace is often much more pervasive than litigation costs. Mistreatment in the workplace consumes a considerable amount of time and energy that would otherwise be spent on task-related efforts. Research has demonstrated that this lost time translates into declining productivity and profits. Workplace mistreatment leads to lower employee morale with associated costs of employee turnover, risks of unionization, dysfunctional work behavior (e.g., sabotage), and even aggressive reactions, such as workplace violence.

The employees involved also usually experience considerable personal costs. Experiencing mistreatment at work can affect individual's ability to focus and perform his or her job well. The mistreatment often continues to occupy the individual's attention outside of the workplace. Mistreatment can not only affect productivity (and subsequent job retention and rewards), it has also been shown to result in adverse work attitudes and psychological and even physiological strain. Recent evidence shows a link between mistreatment and health outcomes.

There are Ways to Minimize or Prevent Mistreatment

In the words of Ben Franklin, "an ounce of prevention is worth a pound of cure." Implementing the right procedures and practices can help to prevent costly mistreatment in the workplace in the first place. While prevention efforts are not completely fail-proof, and some level of disagreement or conflict is actually desirable (although mistreatment, per se, is not!), there are several ways in which you can prevent mistreatment or minimize its severity in your organization. A particularly important preventive measure is to engage in scanning so that potential and nascent mistreatment issues are addressed early. Prevention methods also include implementing appropriate recruiting, selection, training, and reward systems so that you have employees who know how they should treat one another and are not rewarded for behaviors that might lead to mistreatment. Other preventive measures include focusing on the development of your managers, who by their very role make decisions that often relate to perceptions of mistreatment or perceptions of fair treatment. They are often in a position to possibly stop mistreatment if it should occur. Another important prevention measure is to use discipline and terminations as appropriate to prevent chronic mistreatment.

Effective Dispute Resolution

The costs of mistreatment in the workplace are daunting, yet costly and pervasive mistreatment in an organization is anything but inevitable. There are steps you can take to address mistreatment (when it does occur), thereby minimizing its costs and preventing other instances of it. However, addressing mistreatment to the fullest extent requires analysis, planning, and coordination. It requires recognizing the prevalence of mistreatment (and the various forms that it takes) in your organization, understanding individual preferences for addressing mistreatment, and identifying aspects of your organization that may uniquely facilitate or hinder effective resolution. In addition, it is important that your organization should incorporate employee voice in the design of a dispute resolution system and identify the goals it hopes to accomplish by implementing a system.

There are a number of dispute resolution systems that can address some aspects of mistreatment, including such well-known approaches as informal discussion, open-door systems, mediation, ombudspersons, and multi-step appeal procedures. Each of these individual approaches has its own set of strengths and weaknesses and may be modified according to your organization's resources and needs. Ideally, however, you should pursue the development of a dispute resolution system that allows you to prevent further mistreatment by offering a variety of approaches for addressing it, that deals with the post-dispute work relationship between those involved in the mistreatment, and that is well integrated with other systems in your organization. This approach is consistent with the best evidence-based practice today; it will allow your organization to combat mistreatment in the workplace in the most effective way possible.

Evaluation and Continuous Improvement of Your Dispute Resolution System

The best way to approach your dispute resolution system is to consider it to be a work in progress. Whether your goal for this system is for it to:

• address workplace mistreatment effectively when it occurs, or
• be perceived as fair by those who use it or don't use it, or

- be cost-effective, or
- handle a broad range of issues for a broad range of individuals

You will need to continuously collect data related to your system's success in meeting any or all of these goals. Earlier we described a number of different types of data you might collect to evaluate the performance of your system, including organizational-level data (e.g., litigation rates), process measures (e.g., average length of time spent resolving a mistreatment), and individual measures (e.g., individuals' evaluations of experience with the system). These data need to be carefully collected from various constituents (e.g., users, non-users, those who felt mistreated, those accused of mistreatment) and evaluated with respect to your organization's goals. Not only will this auditing allow you to modify and further improve your system, it will also provide valuable information about your organization's policies/procedures, workplace practices, and culture.

Beyond Dispute Resolution

Arguably the most important thing to remember is that employees who have been involved in an incident of workplace mistreatment are, well, *human*. Just because a peer review panel has made a final decision about a claim of mistreatment, or both parties have reached an agreement, or one party (or both!) has left the organization, does not mean the effects of the mistreatment will stop. Feeling mistreated or being accused of mistreating others is hardly a pleasant experience and may be quite difficult to "shake off." Indeed, the relationship between the parties, as well as coworkers, and others who might have engaged in sense-making with the individuals involved will continue to be affected by the situation. One or both parties may feel angry, disappointed, or awkward with one another. These emotional reactions of one party may then be picked up and noticed by the other party, who may react to this reaction, thereby contributing to a spiral of mistreatment.

It is critically important to address the post-mistreatment relationship between the parties and others to stem additional incidents of mistreatment. This may be fairly simple to do, perhaps with an informal discussion between the parties or a facilitated discussion with a third party. Or it may require someone with clinical expertise who can address the process of repairing the relationship. Sometimes a relationship may not be reparable, and one or both individuals may need to be moved. Likewise, some individuals may continue to feel mistreated after the available resources have been exhausted. In situations like these where individuals are still not satisfied with the outcome, it is paramount to continue to practice the principles of both procedural justice and interactional justice to mitigate the negative consequences.

Conclusion

Our understanding of how individuals reach conclusions that they have been mistreated at work and of how this mistreatment can be fully addressed by carefully designed dispute resolution procedures, particularly comprehensive systems, has grown considerably over the past few decades. We know from evidence-based best practices and research that, with the right systems and attention, most mistreatment perceptions *can* be fully addressed within the organization. Furthermore, the incidence of mistreatment can be minimized through the implementation of state-of-the art human resource practices in selection, training, compensation, discipline, and development. Although such state-of-the-art practices will not ensure that *all* mistreatment issues will be handled internally, they go a long way toward not only minimizing and addressing mistreatment, but also toward improving your organization's functioning overall.

Notes

Chapter 1: Introduction

1 Keashly and Jagatic, 2000.
2 Pearson, Andersson, and Wegner, 2001; Keashly and Neuman, 2002; Rayner and Cooper, 2006.
3 Grubb, 2006.
4 http://www.eeoc.gov/stats/charges.html, accessed March 25, 2008.
5 Lewin, 1987; Lewin and Peterson, 1988 and 1999.
6 Hom and Griffeth, 1995. .
7 Bliss, W.G. *Cost of Employee Turnover*. http://www.isquare.com/turnover.cfm, accessed January 28, 2008.
8 Herscovis and Barling, 2006.
9 Tepper, 2000a and 2000b.

Chapter 2: Concluding Mistreatment

1 Greenberg, 1987; Colquitt and Greenberg, 2005.
2 Leventhal, Karuza, and Fry, 1980.
3 Pearson, Andersson, and Wegner, 2001.
4 Rayner and Cooper, 2006.
5 Rayner and Cooper, 2006.
6 Miceli and Near, 1992; Near and Miceli, 1995.
7 http://m-w.com/cgi-bin/dictionary?va=harass, accessed June 6, 2007.
8 http://www.eeoc.gov/types/harassment.html, accessed March 25th, 2008
9 http://www.eeoc.gov/stats/harassment.html, accessed March 25th, 2008.
10 http://www.eeoc.gov/facts/fs-sex.html, accessed June 6, 2007.

11 EEOC: http://www.eeoc.gov/stats/harass.html
12 Sidanius and Pratto, 1999.
13 Bennett-Alexander and Hartman, 2003.
14 Wheller, Klaas, and Rojot, 1994; Colvin, 2006.
15 Koppel, 2007.
16 *Gilmer v. Interstate/Johnson Lane Corp.* (1991). 500 U.S. 20, 26, 111 S.Ct. 1647, 1652; *Circuit City Stores, Inc. v. Adams* (2001) 532 U.S. 105, 122–123, 121 S.Ct. 1302, 1313.
17 Volkema, Farquhar, and Bergmann, 1996.
18 Volkema, Farquhar, and Bergmann, 1996.

Chapter 3: Workplace Scanning for Potential, Nascent, and Existent Mistreatment Issues

1 Hirschman, 1970.
2 Harlos, 2001.
3 Riordan, Vandenberg, and Richardson, 2005.
4 Kaminski, 1999.
5 O'Reilly and Pfeffer, 2000: p128.
6 O'Reilly and Pfeffer, 2000: p. 130.

Chapter 4: Preventing Mistreatment through Workplace Practices

1 Truxillo and Bauer, 1999; Truxillo, Bauer, and Sanchez, 2001; Truxillo, Bauer, Campion, and Paronto, 2002.
2 Boswell, Roehling, LePine, and Moynihan, 2003.
3 Rousseau, 1995.
4 Gatewood, Field, and Barrick, 2008; Heneman and Judge, 2008.
5 Goldberg, 1990.
6 Wernimont and Campbell, 1968; Owens and Schoenfeldt, 1979.
7 Janz, 1982.
8 Hunter and Hunter, 1984; Dipboye, Wooten, and Halverson, 2004.
9 Taylor, Pajo, Cheung, and Stringfield, 2004; Zimmerman, Triana, and Barrick (n.d.).
10 Goldberg, *et al.*, 1991.
11 Allen, Poteet, and Finkelstein, in progress.
12 Noe, 2005.
13 Noe, 2005.
14 Hemphill and Haines, 1997.
15 Sutton, 2007.

16 Kerr, 1975.
17 Mueller, Iverson, and Jo, 1999; Herscovis and Barling, 2006.
18 Liden, Sparrowe, and Wayne, 1997.
19 Burns, 1978; Bass, 1985.
20 Herscovis and Barling, 2006.

Chapter 5: Getting Started on Designing Effective Dispute Resolution Systems

1 Weiss and Cropanzano, 1996; Fiske and Taylor, 1991; Frone, 2000; Spector and Jex, 1998; Cortina *et al.*, 2001; Lim and Cortina, 2005.
2 Weiss and Cropanzano, 1996.

Chapter 6: Dispute Resolution System Options

1 Singer, 1992.
2 Arnold and O'Connor, 1999.
3 http://www.colorado.gov/dpa/mediation/, accessed January 22, 2008.
4 http://www.eeoc.gov/mediate/history.html, accessed January 22, 2008.
5 http://www.stanford.edu/dept/ombuds/how_we_help.html,   accessed January 22, 2008.
6 Slaikeu and Hasson, 1998.
7 http://www.ombudsassociation.org/;   http://web.mit.edu/negotiation/toa/TOAintro.html; http://www.usombudsman.org/, accessed January 22, 2008
8 Lipsky, Seeber, and Fincher, 2003.
9 http://www.policy.ilstu.edu/policydocs/ap_ethics.htm
10 http://www.okdhs.org/library/policy/dhs/002/01/0152000.htm
11 http://money.cnn.com/2007/05/24/news/companies/pluggedin_gunther_marriott.fortune/index.htm
12 Wilensky and Jones, 1994.
13 http://www.adr.org/arb_med, accessed January 22, 2008.
14 Greenberg, 1990.

Chapter 7: Contemporary Best Practices: State-of-the-Art Dispute Resolution Systems

1 Slaikeu and Hasson, 1992.
2 Lipsky, Seeber, and Fincher, 2003.
3 Bendersky, 2003.

4 Brockner and Wiesenfeld, 1996.
5 Leventhal, Karuza, and Fry, 1980.

Chapter 8: Evaluating, Modifying, and Learning from Dispute Resolution Systems

1 Colquitt, 2001.
2 Colvin, 2004.

Chapter 9: Repairing or Addressing the Disputants' Relationship

1 Dupre, 2004.
2 Aquino *et al.*, 2003.
3 Exline *et al.*, 2003.
4 Lewicki and Bunker, 1996; Freedman, 1998; Aquino *et al.*, 2003; Tomlinson, Dineen, and Lewicki, 2004.
5 Lewicki and Bunker, 1996; Freedman, 1998; Tomlinson, Dineen, and Lewicki, 2004.
6 Aquino, Tripp, and Bies, 2001.
7 Tomlinson, Dineen, and Lewicki, 2004.
8 Rousseau *et al.*, 1998.
9 Schweitzer, Hershey, and Bradlow, 2006.
10 Suffolk University, College of Arts and Sciences, Center for Restorative Justice website (http://www.suffolk.edu/research/6953.html), accessed January 14, 2008.

Further Reading and References

Allen, T. D., Poteet, M. L., and Finkelstein, L. (in progress). *Designing Effective Mentoring Programs*. Oxford: Blackwell-Wiley Publishing.

Aquino, K., Grover, S. L., Goldman, B., and Folger, R. (2003). When push doesn't come to shove: Interpersonal forgiveness in workplace relationships. *Journal of Management Inquiry*, 12, 209–16.

Aquino, K., Tripp, T., and Bies, R. (2001). How employees respond to personal offense: The effects of blame attribution, victim status, and offender status on revenge and reconciliation in the workplace. *Journal of Applied Psychology*, 86, 52–9.

Arnold, J. A. and O'Connor, K. M. (1999). Ombudspersons or peers? The effect of third-party expertise and recommendations on negotiation. *Journal of Applied Psychology*, 84, 776–85.

Bass, B. M. (1985). *Leadership and Performance Beyond Expectations*. New York: Free Press.

Bendersky, C. (2003). Organizational dispute resolution systems: A complementarities model. *Academy of Management Review*, 28, 643–56.

Bennett-Alexander, D. D. and Hartman, L. P. (2003). *Employment Law for Business* (5th edition). New York: McGraw-Hill Irwin.

Bergmann, T. J. and Volkema, R. J. (1994). Issues, behavioral responses and consequences in interpersonal conflicts. *Journal of Organizational Behavior*, 15, 467–71.

Bies, R. J. and Shapiro, D. L. (1988). Voice and justification: Their influence on procedural fairness judgments. *Academy of Management Journal*, 31, 676–85.

Boswell, W. R., Boudreau, J. W., and Tichy, J. (2005). The relationship between employee job change and job satisfaction: The honeymoon-hangover effect. *Journal of Applied Psychology*, 90, 882–92.

Boswell, W. R. and Olson-Buchanan, J. B. (2004). Experiencing mistreatment at work: The role of grievance-filing, nature of mistreatment, and employee withdrawal. *Academy of Management Journal*, 47, 129–39.

Boswell, W. R., Roehling, M. V., LePine, M. A., and Moynihan, L. M. (2003). Individual job choice decisions and the impact of job attributes and recruitment practices: A longitudinal field study. *Human Resource Management*, 42, 23–37.

Boswell, W. R., Shipp, A. J., Payne, S. C., and Youngcourt, S. S. (2008) *Changes in Job Satisfaction: A Longitudinal Study of Organizational Newcomers*. Paper presented at the 23rd annual meeting of the Society for Industrial and Organizational Psychology, San Francisco, CA, April.

Braverman, M. (1999). *Preventing Workplace Violence: A Guide for Employers and Practitioners*. Thousand Oaks, CA: Sage Publications, Inc.

Brockner, J. and Wiesenfeld, B. M. (1996). An integrative framework for explaining reactions to decisions: The interactive effects of outcomes and procedures. *Psychological Bulletin*, 120, 189–208.

Burns, J. M. (1978). *Leadership*. New York: Harper and Row.

Colquitt, J. A. (2001). On the dimensionality of organizational justice: A construct validation of a measure. *Journal of Applied Psychology*, 86, 386–400.

Colquitt, J. A. and Greenberg, J. (2005). *Handbook of Organizational Justice*. Mahwah, NJ: Lawrence Erlbaum Associates Publishers.

Colvin, A. J. S. (2004). Adoption and use of dispute resolution procedures in the nonunion workplace. *Advances in Industrial and Labor Relations*, 13, 69–95.

Colvin, A. J. S. (2003). Institutional pressures, human resource strategies and the rise of nonunion dispute resolution procedures. *Industrial and Labor Relations Review*, 56, 375–92.

Cortina, L. M. and Magley, V. J. (2003). Raising voice, risking retaliation: Events following interpersonal mistreatment in the workplace. *Journal of Occupational Health Psychology*, 8, 247–65.

Cortina, L. M., Magley, V. J., Williams, J. H., and Langhout, R. D. (2001). Incivility in the workplace: Incidence and impact. *Journal of Occupational Health Psychology*, 6, 64–80.

Costantino, C. A. and Merchant, C. S. (1996). *Designing Conflict Management Systems: A Guide to Creating Productive and Healthy Organizations*. San Francisco, CA: Jossey-Bass.

Cropanzano, R. (ed.) (2001). *Justice in the Workplace: From Theory to Practice*. Mahwah, N.J.: Lawrence Erlbaum Associates.

Degoey, P. (2000). Contagious justice: Exploring the social construction of justice in organizations. *Research in Organizational Behavior*, 22, 51–103.

Deutsch, M. (1973). *The Resolution of Conflict: Constructive and Destructive Processes.* New Haven, CT: Yale University Press.

Dibble, R. E. (1997). Alternative dispute resolution of employment conflict: The search for standards. *Journal of Collective Negotiations,* 26, 73–84.

Dipboye, R. L., Wooten, K., and Halverson, S. K. (2004). Behavioral and situational interviews. In J. C. Thomas (ed.), *Comprehensive Handbook of Psychological Assessment* (pp. 297–316). Hoboken, NJ: John Wiley and Sons.

Dupre, K. E. (2004) "Beating Up the Boss: The Prediction and Prevention of Interpersonal Aggression Targeting Supervisors." Unpublished Dissertation. Queens University, Kingston, Canada.

Einarsen, S., Hoel, H., Zapf, D., and Cooper, C. L. (2003). *Bullying and Emotional Abuse in the Workplace: International Perspectives on Research and Practice.* New York: Taylor and Francis.

Exline, J. J., Worthington, E. L., Hill, P., and McCullough, M. E. (2003). Forgiveness and justice: A research agenda for social and personality psychology. *Personality and Social Psychology Review,* 4, 337–48.

Fine, M. (1979). Options to injustice: Seeing other lights. *Representative Research in Social Psychology,* 10, 61–76.

Fiske, S. T. and Taylor, S. E. (1991). *Social Cognition* (2nd edition). McGraw-Hill series in social psychology. New York: McGraw-Hill Book Company.

Folger J. P. and Poole, M. S. (1984). *Working through Conflict: A Communication Perspective.* Glenview, IL: Scott Foresman.

Folger, R., and Greenberg, J. (1985). Procedural justice: An interpretive analysis of personnel systems. In K. Rowland and G. Ferris (eds.), *Research in Personnel and Human Resource Management* (Vol. 3, pp. 141–83). Greenwich, CT: JAI Press.

Freedman, S. (1998). Forgiveness and reconciliation: The importance of understanding how they differ. *Counseling and Values,* 42, 200–16.

Freeman, R. B. (1980). The exit-voice tradeoff in the labor market: Unionism, job tenure, quits, and separations. *Quarterly Journal of Economics,* 94, 643–73.

Frone, M. (2000). Interpersonal conflict at work and psychological outcomes: Testing a model among young workers. *Journal of Occupational Health Psychology,* 5, 246–55.

Gatewood, R. D., Field, H. S., and Barrick, M. (2008), *Human Resource Selection.* South-Western College Publications.

Goldberg, L. R. (1990). An alternative "description of personality": The Big-Five factor structure. *Journal of Personality and Social Psychology,* 59, 1216–229.

Goldberg, L. R., Grenier, J. R., Guion, L. B., Sechrest, L. B., and Wing, H. (1991). *Questionnaires Used in the Prediction of Trustworthiness in Pre-Employment Selection Decisions.* An APA Task Force Report, Washington, DC: American Psychological Association.

Greenberg, J. (1987). Reactions to procedural justice in pay distributions: Do the means justify the ends? *Journal of Applied Psychology*, 72, 55–61.

Greenberg, J. (1990). Organizational justice; yesterday, today, and tomorrow. *Journal of Management*, 16, 399–432.

Griffin, R. W., O'Leary-Kelly, A., and L. M. Collins (eds.). (1998). *Dysfunctional Behavior in Organizations: Violent and Deviant Behavior.* Greenwich, CT: Elsevier Science/JAI Press.

Grubb, P. (2006). *Workplace Bullying: Current Research and Next Steps.* Paper presented as part of the symposium "Building a Research and Prevention Initiative for Workplace Violence." Work, Stress, and Health Conference, Miami, FL.

Haines, R. and Hemphill, H. (1997). *Discrimination, Harassment, and the Failure of Diversity Training.* Westport, CT: Quorum Books.

Harlos, K. P. (2001). When organizational voice systems fail: More on the deaf-ear syndrome and frustration effects. *Journal of Applied Behavioral Science*, 37, 324–42.

Heneman, H. G. and Judge, T. A. (2008). *Staffing Organizations.* New York: Irwin/McGraw-Hill.

Herscovis, M. S. and Barling, J. (2006). Preventing insider-initiated workplace violence. In E. K. Kelloway, J. Barling, and J. J. Hurrell Jr. (eds.), *Handbook of Workplace Violence* (pp. 607–32). Thousand Oaks, CA: Sage Publications, Inc.

Hirschman, A. O. (1970). *Exit, Voice, and Loyalty.* Cambridge, MA: Harvard University Press.

Hom, P. W. and Griffeth, R. W. (1995). *Employee Turnover.* Cincinnati, OH: Southwestern Publishing.

Horsbrugh, H. J. N. (1974). Forgiveness. *Canadian Journal of Philosophy*, 4, 269–82.

Houlden, P., LaTour, S., Walker, L., and Thibaut, J. (1978). Preference for modes of dispute resolution as a function of process and decision control. *Experimental Social Psychology*, 14, 13–30.

Hunter, J. E. and Hunter, R. F. (1984). Validity and utility of alternative predictors of job performance. *Psychological Bulletin*, 96, 72–98.

Jameson, J. K. (1999). Toward a comprehensive model for the assessment and management of intraorganizational conflict: Developing the framework. *The International Journal of Conflict Management*, 10, 268–94.

Janz, T. (1982). Initial comparisons of patterned behavior description interviews versus unstructured interviews. *Journal of Applied Psychology*, 67, 577–80.

Jehn, K. A. (1995). A multi-method examination of the benefits and detriments of intra-group conflict. *Administrative Science Quarterly*, 40, 256–82.

Johnstone, G. and Van Ness, D. W. (2007). *Handbook of Restorative Justice*. Cullompton, Devon, UK: Willan Publishing.

Kaminski, M. (1999). New forms of work organization and their impact on the grievance procedure. In E. Eaton and J. H. Keefe (eds.), *Employment Dispute Resolution and Worker Rights* (pp. 219–46). Champaign, IL: Industrial Relations Research Association.

Keashly, L. and Neuman, J. H. (2002). *Exploring Persistent Patterns of Workplace Aggression*. Paper presented as part of symposium "Workplace Abuse, Aggression, Bullying, and Incivility: Conceptual Integration and Empirical Insights," Annual meeting of the Academy of Management, Denver, CO.

Keashly, L. and Jagatic, K. (2000). *The Nature, Extent and Impact of Emotional Abuse in the Workplace: Results of a Statewide Survey*. Paper presented at the Academy of Management Conference, Toronto, Canada in August 2000.

Kerr, S. (1975). On the folly of rewarding A, while hoping for B. *Academy of Management Journal*, 18, 769–83.

Klaas, B. S. (1989). Determinants of grievance activity and the grievance system's impact on employee behavior: An integrative perspective. *Academy of Management Review*, 14, 445–58.

Klaas, B. S. and DeNisi, A. S. (1989). Managerial reactions to employee dissent: The impact of grievance activity on performance ratings. *Academy of Management Journal*, 32, 705–18.

Koppel, N. (2007). Getting Ready to Sue the Boss? Not So Fast. *Wall Street Journal*, December 30, 2007.

Leventhal, G. S., Karuza, J., and Fry, W. R. (1980). Beyond fairness: A theory of allocation preferences. In G. Mikula (ed.), *Justice and Social Interaction*: 167–218. New York: Springer-Verlag.

Lewicki, R. J. and Bunker, B. B. (1996). Developing and maintaining trust in work relationships. In R. M. Kramer, and T. R. Tyler (eds.), *Trust in Organizations: Frontiers of Theory and Research* (pp. 114–39). Thousand Oaks, CA; Sage Publications, Inc.

Lewin, D. (1987). Conflict resolution in the nonunion firm: A theoretical and empirical analysis. *Journal of Conflict Resolution*, 31, 465–502.

Lewin, D., and Peterson, R. B. (1999). Behavioral outcomes of grievance activity. *Industrial Relations*, 38, 554–76.

Lewin, D. and Peterson, R. B. (1988). *The Modern Grievance Procedure in the United States: A Theoretical and Empirical Analysis*. Westport, CT: Quorum.

Liden, R. C., Sparrowe, R. T., and Wayne, S. J. (1997). Leader-member exchange theory: The past and potential for the future. *Research in Personnel and Human Resource Management*, 15, 47–119.

Lim, S. and Cortina, L. M. (2005). Interpersonal mistreatment in the workplace: The interface and impact of general incivility and sexual harassment. *Journal of Applied Psychology*, 90, 483–96.

Lipsky, D. B., Seeber, R. L., and Fincher, R. (2003). *Emerging Systems for Managing Workplace Conflict*. San Francisco, CA: Jossey-Bass.

Miceli, M. P. and Near, J. P. (1992). *Blowing the Whistle: The Organizational and Legal Implications for Companies and Employees*. New York: Lexington.

Mueller, C. W., Iverson, R. D., and Jo, D. G., (1999). Distributive justice evaluations in two cultural contexts: A comparison of U.S. and South Korean teachers, *Human Relations*, 52, 869–93.

Near, J. P. and Miceli, M. P. (1995). Effective whistle-blowing. *Academy of Management Review*, 20, 679–708.

Needham, A. W. (2004). *Workplace Bullying: A Costly Business Secret*. Auckland: Penguin Global.

Noe, R. A. (2005). *Employee Training and Development*. Boston, MA: Irwin McGraw-Hill.

North, J. (1987). Wrongdoing and forgiveness. *Philosophy*, 62, 499–508.

Olson-Buchanan, J. B. (1997). To grieve or not to grieve? Factors related to voicing discontent in an organizational simulation. *The International Journal for Conflict Management*, 8(2), 132–47.

Olson-Buchanan, J. B. (1996). Voicing discontent: What happens to the grievance filer after the grievance. *Journal of Applied Psychology*, 81, 52–63.

Olson-Buchanan, J. B. and Boswell, W. R. (2008). An integrative model of experiencing and responding to mistreatment at work. *Academy of Management Review*, 33, 76–96.

Olson-Buchanan, J. B. and Boswell, W. R. (2006). Blurring boundaries: Correlates of integration and segmentation between work and nonwork. *Journal of Vocational Behavior*, 68, 432–45.

Olson-Buchanan, J. B. and Boswell, W. R. (2002). The role of employee loyalty and formality in voicing discontent. *Journal of Applied Psychology*, 87, 1167–74.

O'Reilly, C. A. and Pfeffer, J. (2000). *Hidden Value: How Great Companies Achieve Extraordinary Results with Ordinary People*. Harvard Business School Press, Boston, MA.

Owens, W. A., and Schoenfeldt, L. F. (1979). Toward a classification of persons. *Journal of Applied Psychology*, 63, 569–607.

Pearson, C. M., Andersson, L. M., and Wegner, J. W. (2001). When workers flout convention: A study of workplace incivility. *Human Relations*, 54, 1397–419.

Peirce, R. S., Pruitt, D. G., and Czaja, S. J. (1993). Complainant–respondent differences in procedural choice. *International Journal of Conflict Management*, 4, 199–222.

Pondy, L. R. (1967). Organizational conflict: Concepts and models. *Administrative Science Quarterly*, 12, 296–320.

Prein, H. (1987). Strategies for third party intervention. *Human Relations*, 40, 699–719.

Pruitt, D., and Rubin, J. Z. (1986). *Social Conflict: Escalation, Stalemate, and Settlement*. New York: Newberry Award Records.

Rahim, M. A. (1986). Referent role and styles of handling interpersonal conflict. *Journal of Social Psychology*, 126, 79–86.

Rayner, C. and Cooper, C. L. (2006). Workplace bullying. In E. K. Kelloway, J. Barling, and J. J. Hurrell Jr. (eds.), *Handbook of Workplace Violence* (pp. 121–45). Thousand Oaks, CA: Sage Publications, Inc.

Rayner, C., Hoel, H., and Cooper, C. L. (2002). *Workplace Bullying: What Do We Know, Who Is to Blame and What Can We Do?* New York: Taylor and Francis.

Renwick, P. A. (1975). Impact of topic and source of disagreement on conflict management. *Organizational Behavior and Human Performance*, 14, 416–25.

Richards, N. (1988). Forgiveness. *Ethics*, 99, 77–97.

Riordan, C. M., Vandenberg, R. J., and Richardson, H. A. (2005). Employee involvement climate and organizational effectiveness. *Human Resource Management*, 44, 471–88.

Robinson, S. L. (1996). Trust and breach of the psychological contract. *Administrative Science Quarterly*, 41, 574–99.

Robinson, S. L., and Rousseau, D. M. (1994). Violating the psychological contract: Not the exception but the norm. *Journal of Organizational Behavior*, 15, 245–59.

Rousseau, D. M. (1995). *Psychological Contracts in Organizations: Understanding Written and Unwritten Agreements*. Newbury Park, CA: Sage.

Rousseau, D. M., Sitkin, S. B., Burt, R. S., and Camerer, C. (1998). Not so different after all: A cross-discipline view of trust. *Academy of Management Review*, 23, 393–404.

Saunders, D. M., Sheppard, B. H., Knight, V., and Roth, J. (1992). Employee voice to supervisors. *Employee Rights and Responsibilities Journal*, 5, 241–59.

Schweitzer, M. E., Hershey, J. C., and Bradlow, E. T. (2006). Promises and lies: Restoring violated trust. *Organizational Behavior and Human Decision Processes*, 10, 1–19.

Sidanius, J., and Pratto, F. (1999). *Social Dominance: An Intergroup Theory of Social Hierarchy and Oppression*. Cambridge: Cambridge University Press.

Singer, A. W. (1992). Is IBM's open door policy still ajar? *Ethikos and Corporate Conduct Quarterly*. Available at http://www.singerpubs.com/ethikos/html/ibm.html, accessed June 15, 2007.

Sitkin, S. B. and Bies, R. J. (1993). Social accounts in conflict situations: Using explanations to manage conflict. *Human Relations*, 46, 349–70.

Slaikeu, K. A. and Hasson, R. H. (1998). *Controlling the Costs of Conflict: How to Design a System for Your Organization*. San Francisco, CA: John Wiley and Sons.

Spector, P. and Jex, S. (1998). Development of four self-report measures of job stressors and strain: Interpersonal Conflict at Work Scale, Organizational Constraints Scale, Quantitative Workload Inventory, and Physical Symptoms Inventory. *Journal of Occupational Health Psychology*, 3, 356–67.

Steiner, D. D., Skarlicki, D. P., and Gilliand, S. W. (eds.) (2002). *Emerging Perspectives on Managing Organizational Justice*. Greenwich, CT: Information Age Publishing.

Strang, H. (2002). *Repair or Revenge: Victims and Restorative Justice*. Oxford: Oxford University Press.

Sutton, R. I. (2007). *The No Asshole Rule: Building a Civilized Workplace and Surviving One That Isn't*. New York: Business Plus.

Taylor, P. J., Pajo, K., Cheung, G. W., and Stringfield, P. (2004). Dimensionality and validity of a structured telephone reference check procedure. *Personnel Psychology*, 57, 745–72.

Tepper, B. J. (2000a). Abusive supervision in work organizations: Review, synthesis, and research agenda. *Journal of Management*, 33, 261–89.

Tepper, B. J. (2000b). Health consequences of organizational injustice: Tests of main and interactive effects. *Organizational Behavior and Human Decision Processes*, 86, 197–216.

Thomas, K. W. (1976). Conflict and conflict management. In M. Dunnette (ed.), *Handbook of Industrial and Organizational Psychology* (pp. 889–933). Chicago: Rand McNally.

Thomas, K. W. and Kilmann, R. H. (1974). *The Thomas-Kilmann Conflict Mode Instrument*. Tuxedo, NY: Xicom.

Todor, W. D. and Owen, C. L. (1991). Deriving benefits from conflict resolution: A macro-justice approach. *Employee Responsibilities and Rights Journal*, 4, 37–49.

Tomlinson, E. C., Dineen, B. R., and Lewicki, R. J. (2004). The road to reconciliation: Antecedents of victim willingness to reconcile following a broken promise. *Journal of Management*, 30, 165–87.

Truxillo, D. M. and Bauer, T. N. (1999). Applicant reactions to test scores banding in entry-level and promotional contexts. *Journal of Applied Psychology*, 84, 322–339.

Truxillo, D. M., Bauer, T. N., and Sanchez, R. J. (2001). Multiple dimensions of procedural justice: Longitudinal effects on selection system fairness and test-taking self-efficacy. *International Journal of Selection and Assessment*, 9, 336–49.

Truxillo, D. M., Bauer, T. N., Campion, M. A., and Paronto, M. E. (2002). Selection fairness information and applicant reactions: A longitudinal field study. *Journal of Applied Psychology*, 87, 1020–31.

Volkema, R. J. and Bergmann, T. J. (1989). Interpersonal conflict at work: An analysis of behavioral responses. *Human Relations*, 42, 757–70.

Volkema, R. J., Farquhar, K., and Bergmann, T. J. (1996). Third-party sensemaking in interpersonal conflicts at work: A theoretical framework. *Human Relations*, 49, 1437–54.

Weiss, H. M. and Cropanzano, R (1996). Effective events theory: A theoretical discussion of the structure, cause, and consequences of affective experiences at work. In B. M. Staw and L. L. Cummings (eds.), *Research in Organizational Behavior: An Annual Series of Analytical Essays and Critical Reviews* (pp. 1–74). Greenwich, CT: Elsevier Science/JAI Press.

Wernimont, P. F. and Campbell, J. P. (1968) Signs, samples, and criteria. *Journal of Applied Psychology*, 52, 372–6.

Wheller, H. N., Klaas, B. S., and Rojot, J. (1994). Justice at work: An international comparison. *Annals of the American Academy of Political and Social Science*, 536 (*Employee dismissal: Justice at work*), 31–42.

Wilensky, R. and Jones, K. (1994). Quick response: Key to resolving complaints. *HR Magazine*, 39(3), 42–7.

Zimmerman, R. D., Triana, M. C., and Barrick, M. R. The criterion-related validity of a structured letter of reference using multiple raters and multiple performance criteria. Working paper.

Author Index

Authors not mentioned in the text have an "n" number after the page reference. More details will be found on pages 179–82

Subject Index